Thamesford Ontario and Area in Colour Photos, Saving Our History One Photo at a Time

Photography
by Barbara Raué
2015

Series Name:
Cruising Ontario

Book 128: Thamesford and Area

Cover photo: 128 Delatre Street West, Page 24

Series Name: Cruising Ontario
Saving Our History One Photo at a Time in colour photos

Books Available in Alphabetical Order:
Aberfoyle, Acton, Alton, Ancaster, Arthur, Aylmer, Ayr, Bloomingdale, Brantford, Burlington, Caledon, Caledonia, Cambridge, Clifford, Conestogo, Delhi, Dorchester to Aylmer, Drayton, Drumbo, Dundas, Eden Mills, Elmira, Elora, Fergus, Guelph, Hagersville, Hamilton, Hanover, Harriston, Hespeler, Jarvis, Kitchener, Linwood, Listowel, London, Lucknow, Mono, Mount Forest, Neustadt, New Hamburg, Niagara-on-the-Lake, Oakville, Orangeville, Orillia, Owen Sound, Palmerston, Peterborough, Port Elgin, Preston, Rockwood, Seaforth, Sheffield, Shelburne, Simcoe, Southampton, St. Jacobs, St. Thomas, Stoney Creek, Stratford, Tillsonburg, Waterdown, Waterford, Waterloo, Wellesley, Wingham

Book 110:Lucknow,Mitchell
Book 111: Conestogo, Bloomingdale
Book 112: Delhi
Book 113: Waterford
Book 114-116: Waterloo
Book 117-119: Windsor
Book 120-121: Amherstburg
Book 122: Essex
Book 123-124: Kingsville
Book 125-127: Woodstock
Book 128: Thamesford
Book 129: St. Mary's

Other Books by Barbara Raue

Coins of Gold

Arrows, Indians and Love

The Life and Times of Barbara
Volume 1: Inventions That Have Enhanced My Life
Volume 2: Entertainment That I Have Enjoyed
Volume 3: East Coast Trips
Volume 4: Olympics Have Always Intrigued Me
Volume 5: Wonders of the World
Volume 6: Caribbean Cruises We Have Enjoyed
Volume 7: Animals
Volume 8: Storms and Other Major Disasters in My Lifetime
Volume 9: Wars, Terrorist Attacks and Major Disasters

The Cromwell Family Book

Laura Secord Discovered

Daddy Where Are You?

Visit Barbara's website to view all of her books
http://barbararaue.ca

Table of Contents

Oxford County is located in the heart of Southwestern Ontario and is made up of eight lower tier Municipalities. Zorra Township is located at the north-west corner of Oxford County. It is a rural municipality, and was formed in 1975 through the amalgamation of East Nissouri, West Zorra and North Oxford townships. The township includes the communities of Banner, Bennington, Brooksdale, Brown's Corners, Cody's Corners, Dicksons Corners, Dunn's Corner, Embro, Golspie, Granthurst, Harrington, Harrington West, Holiday, **Kintore**, Lakeside, Maplewood, McConkey, **Medina**, Rayside, **Thamesford, Uniondale**, Youngsville, and Zorra Station.

Kintore, Medina, Thamesford and Uniondale are included in this book of photos.

Thamesford is located on the western boundary of Oxford County, half way between London and Woodstock on Highway 2 (County Road 68) and between St. Mary's and Ingersoll on Highway 19.

Thames Centre is a municipality in Middlesex County east of the City of London. It was formed on January 1, 2001, when the townships of West Nissouri and North Dorchester were amalgamated. Communities in the township include: Avon, Belton, Cherry Grove, Crampton, Cobble Hill, Derwent, Devizes, Dorchester, Evelyn, Fanshawe Lake, Friendly Corners, Gladstone, Harrietsville, Kelly Station, Mossley, Nilestown, Oliver, **Putnam**, Salmonville, Silvermoon, Thorndale, Three Bridges, and Wellburn.

Putnam is included in this book of photos.

Thamesford

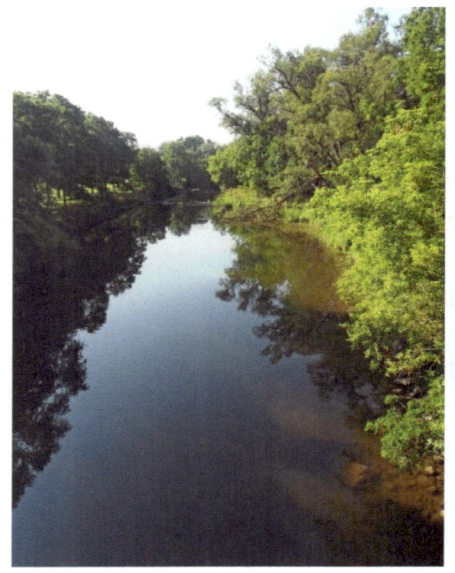
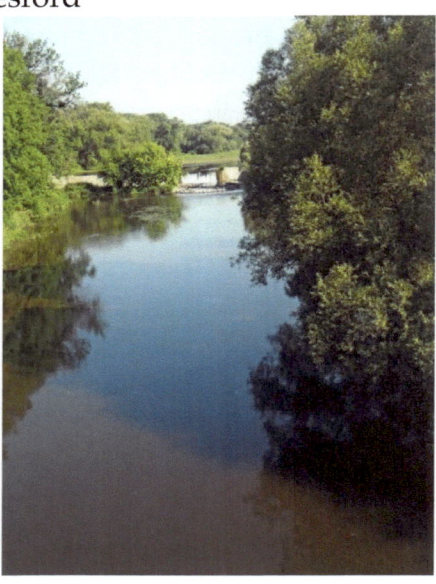

Thames River

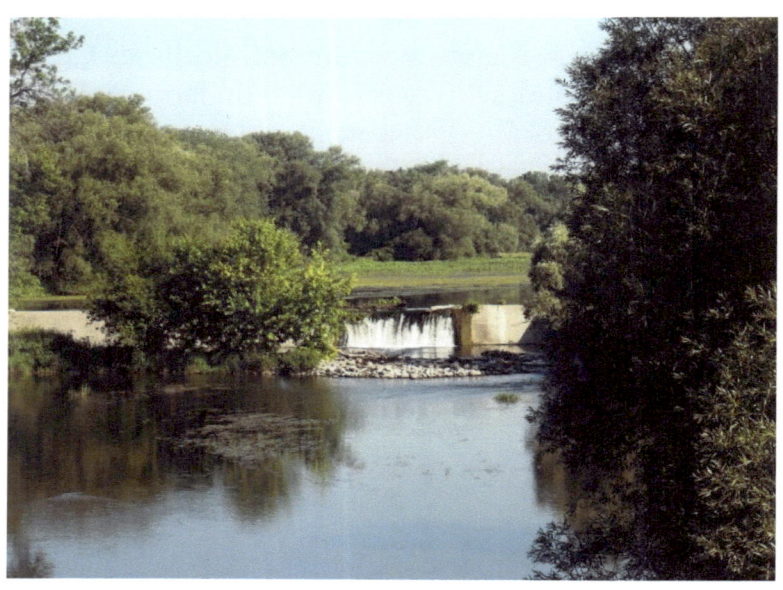

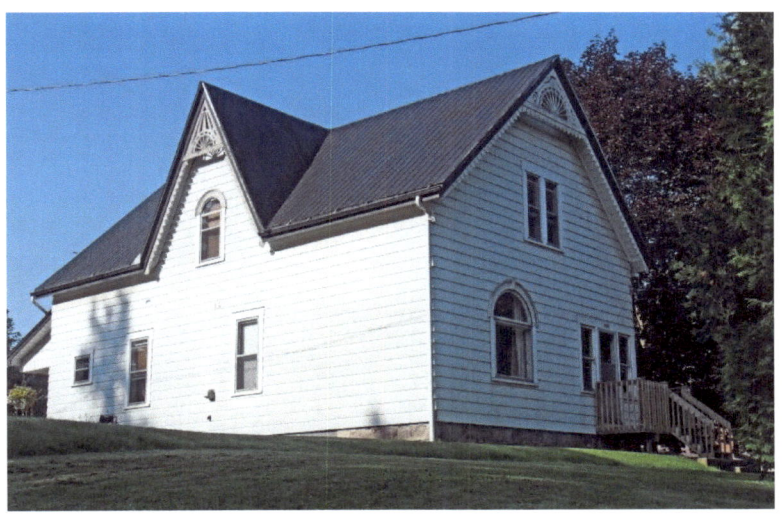

Dundas Street – Gothic Revival - within peak of each gable is a decorative arch with applied scrollwork, spindles & circular piercing

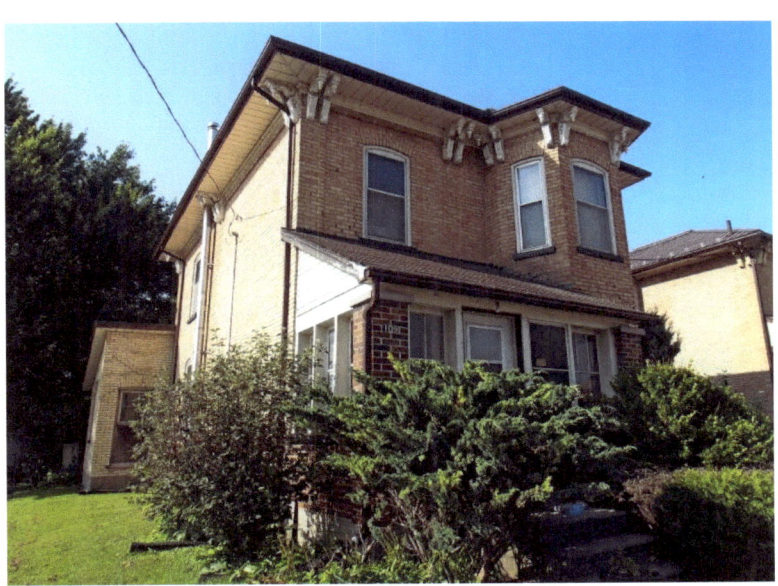

109 Dundas Street – Italianate – paired cornice brackets, second floor bay window

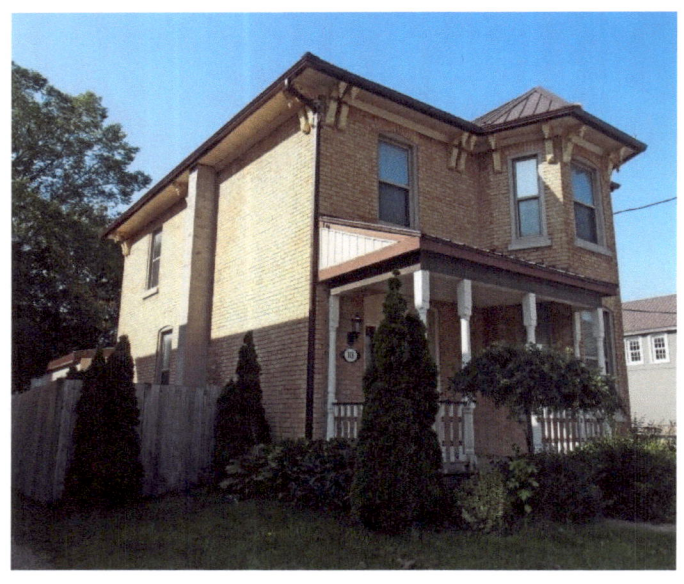

113Dundas Street – Italianate – paired cornice brackets, wood-turned verandah supports

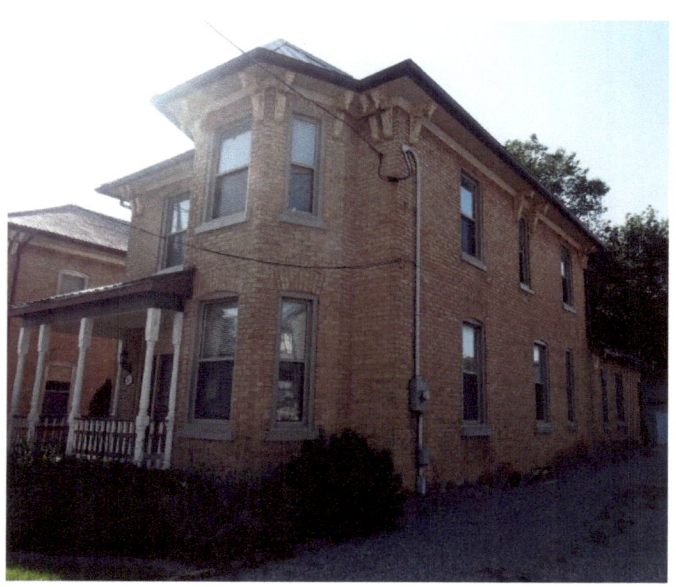

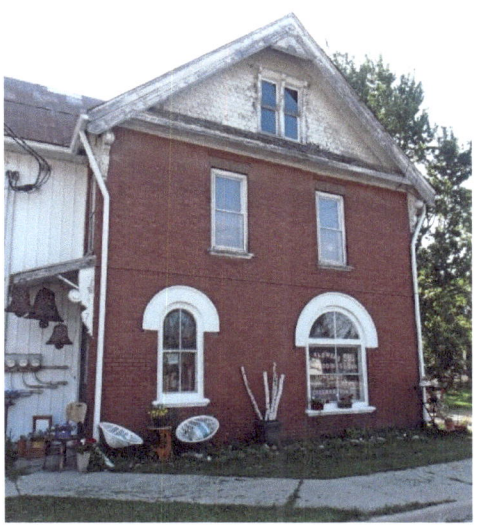

Dundas Street

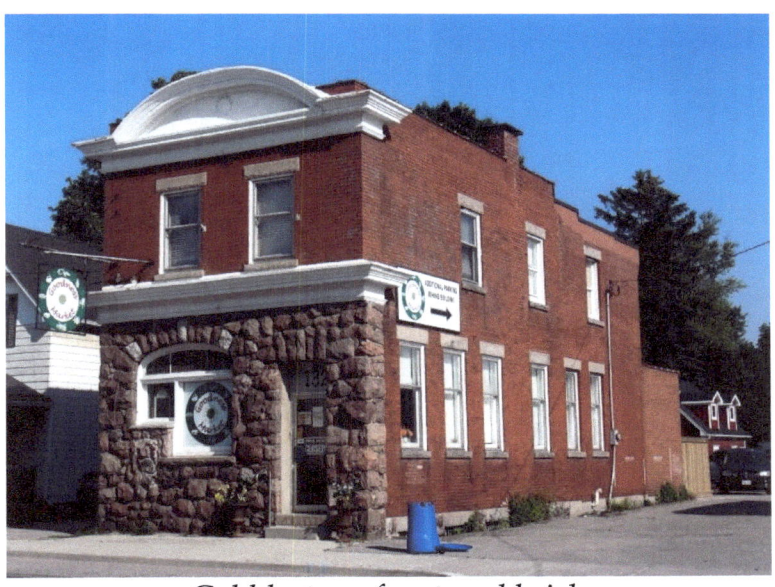

Cobblestone front, red brick

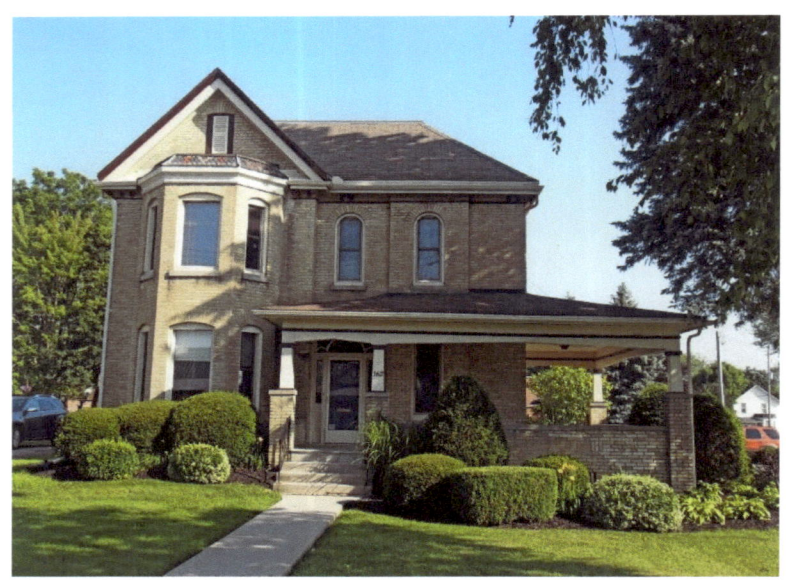

162 Dundas Street – Italianate, hipped roof, two-storey tower-like bay topped with a pediment, wraparound verandah

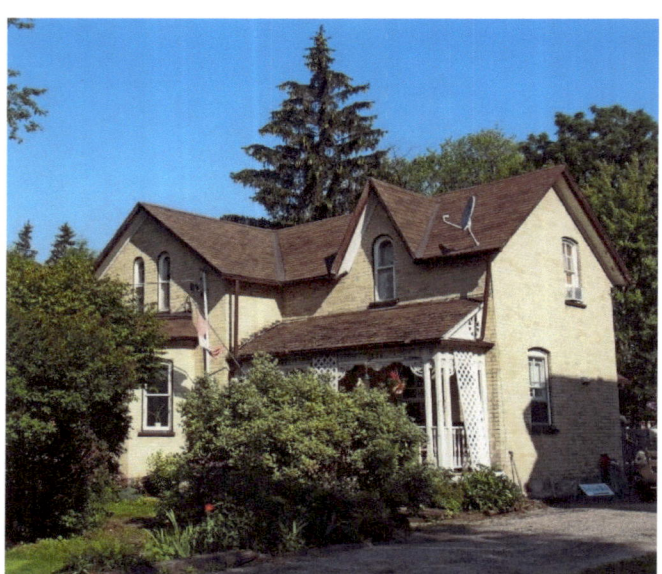

Dundas Street - Gothic Revival

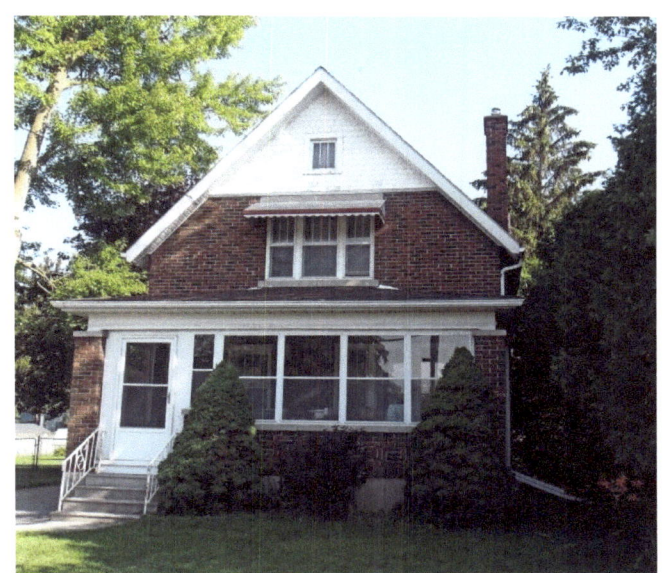

170 Dundas Street - vernacular

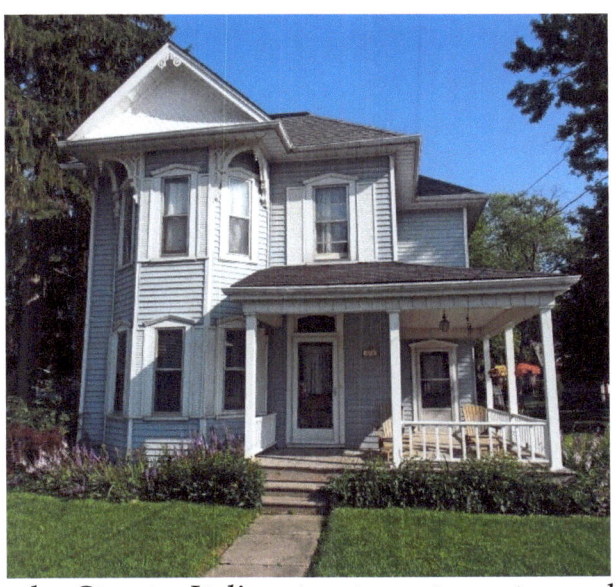

174 Dundas Street – Italianate – two-storey tower-like bay topped with pediment with fish scale pattern, fretwork

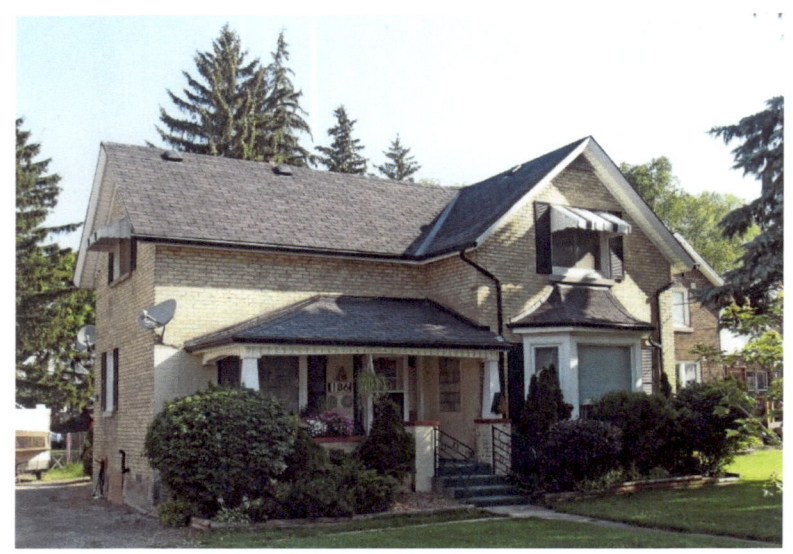

186 Dundas Street

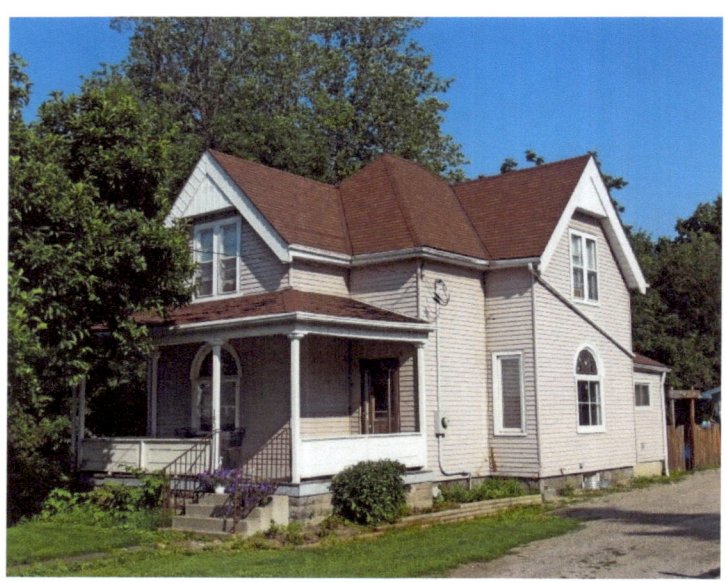

190 Dundas Street

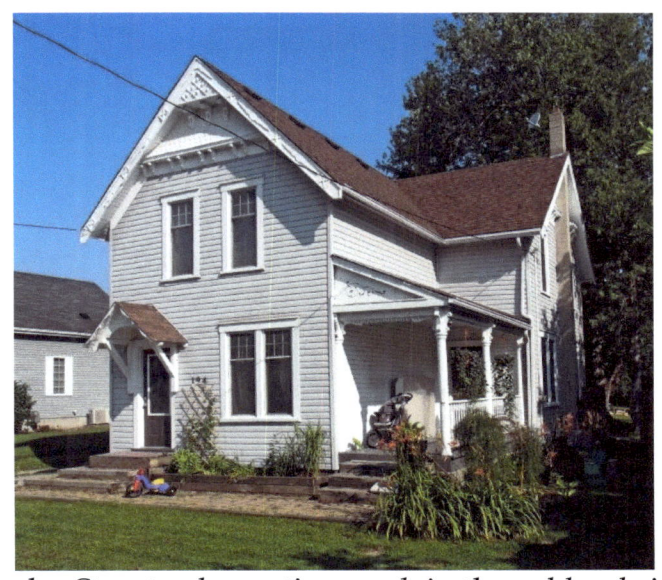

194 Dundas Street – decorative work in the gables, bric-a-brac and stenciling on the porch

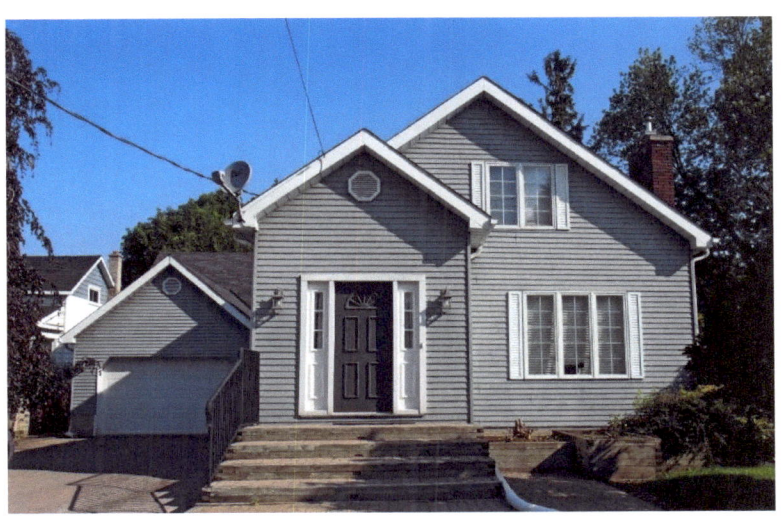

vernacular

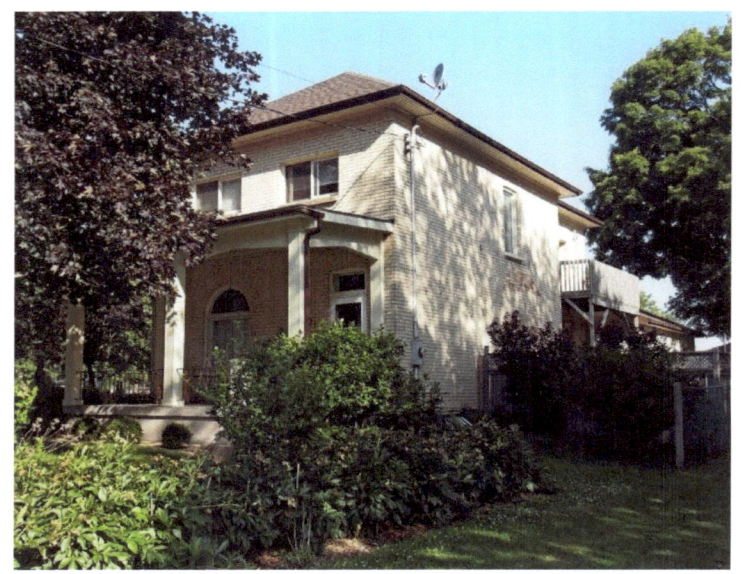

212 Dundas Street – hipped roof

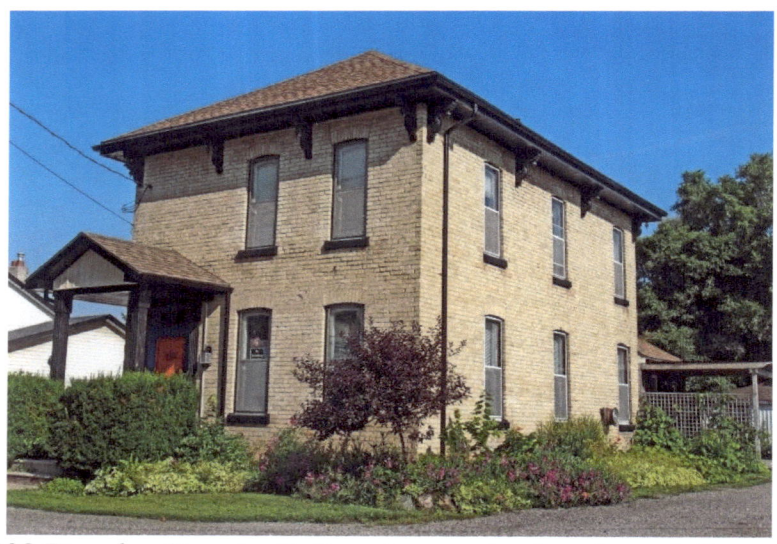

232 Dundas Street – Italianate, cornice brackets, full two-storey building, hipped roof, pediment above porch

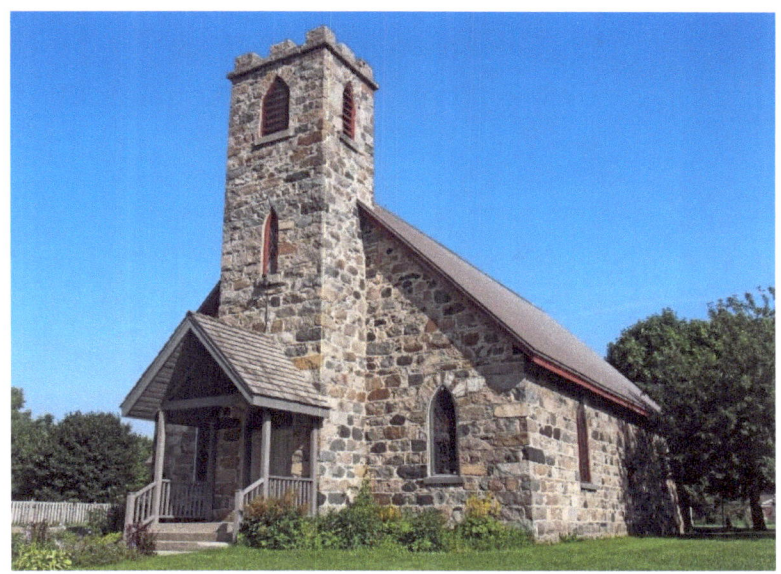

220 Dundas Street West - St. John's Anglican Church – 1861 – Stonemason, John Forbes selected and gathered the stones from John Halpin's farm, one mile south of the village; they were hewn with dexterity and laid with precision. The hand-axed beams and rafters were hewn and drawn from the pinewood lot of Robert Rutledge by Charles Corbin; lancet windows

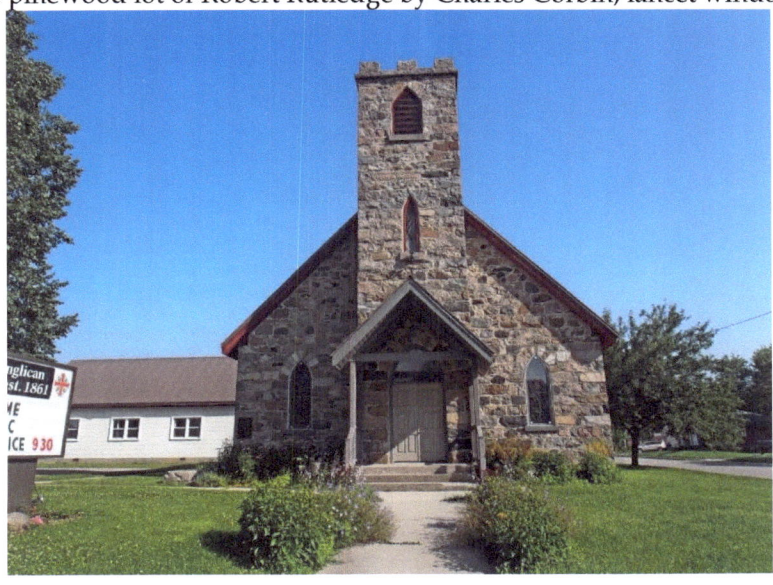

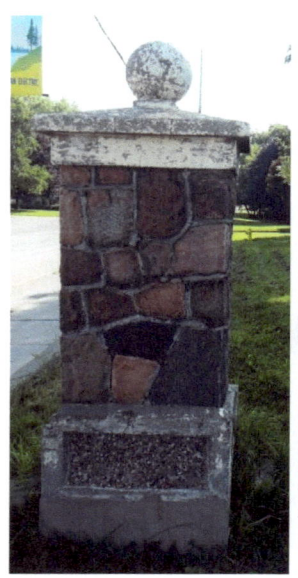 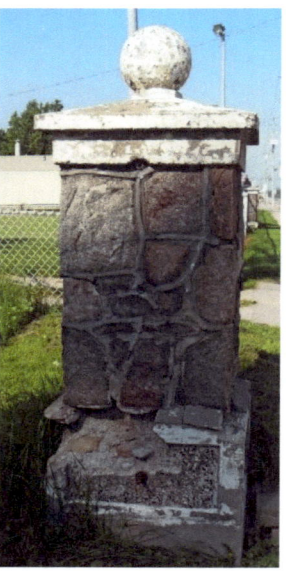

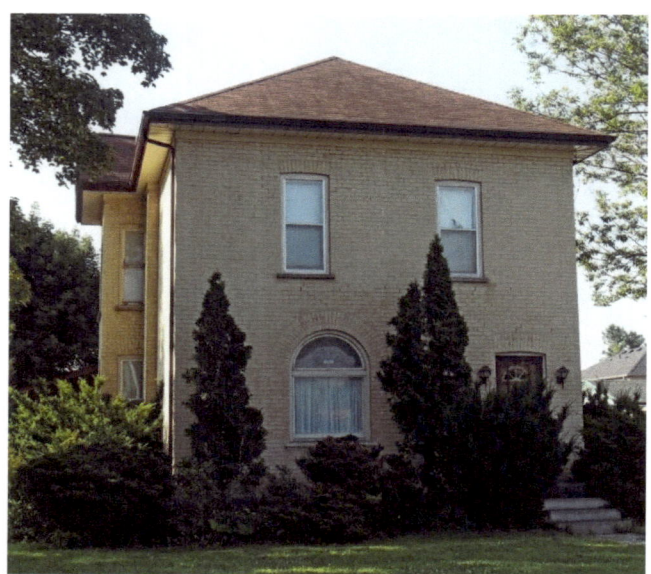

Dundas Street - Italianate, hipped roof

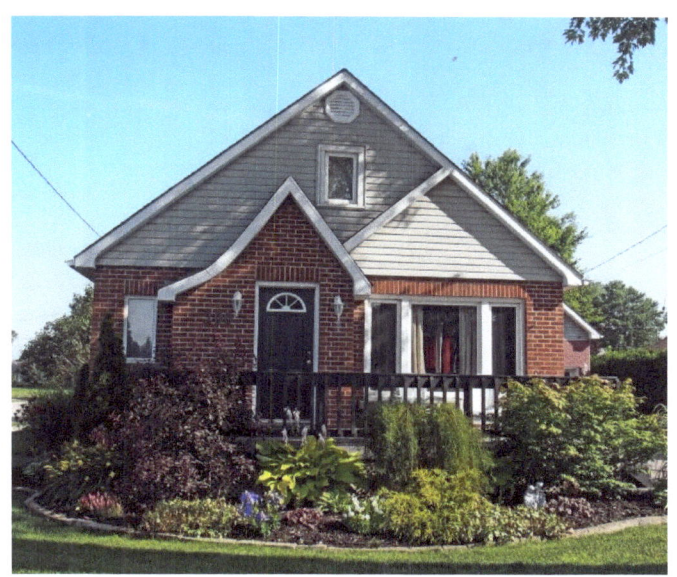

200 Delatre Street West - vernacular

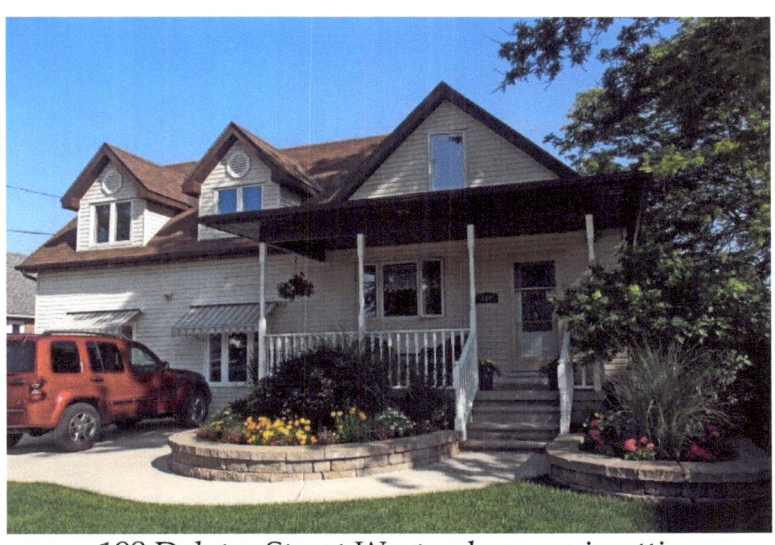

198 Delatre Street West – dormers in attic

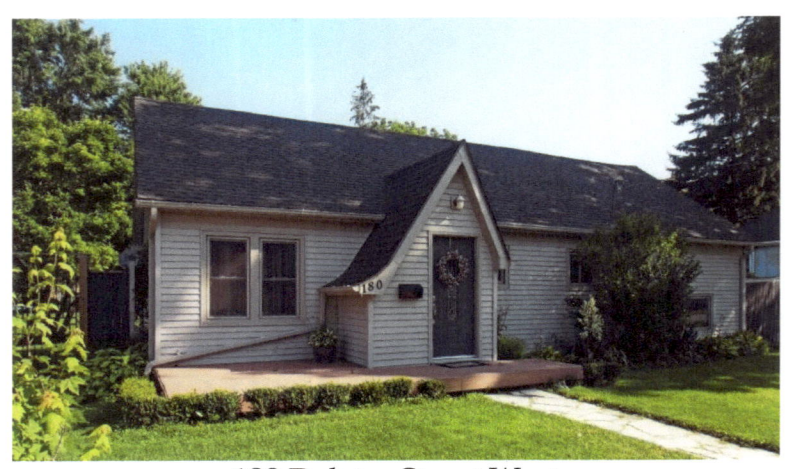

180 Delatre Street West

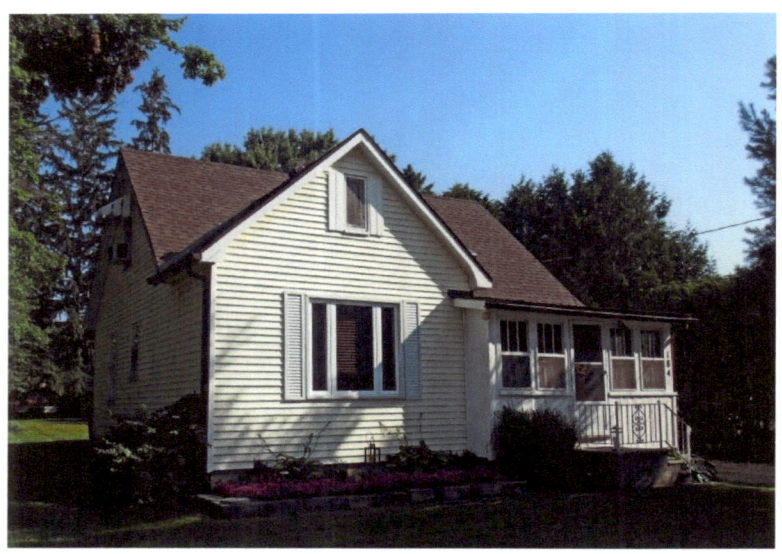

184 Delatre Street West

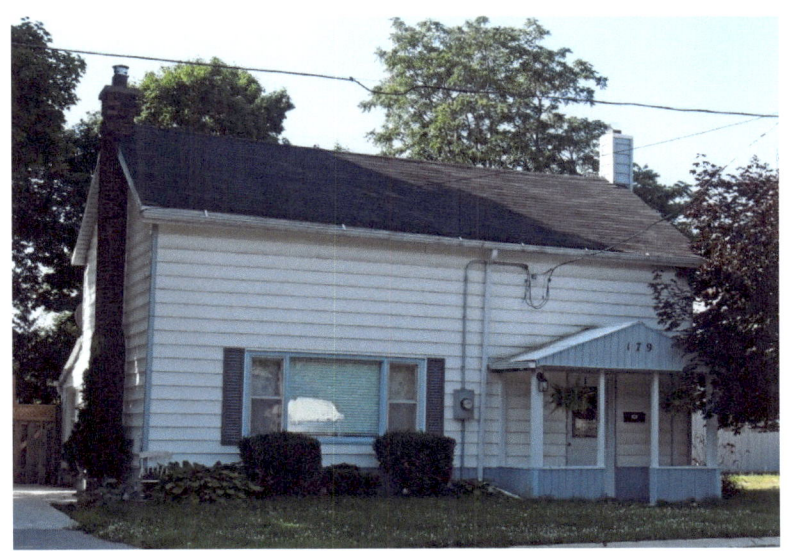

179 Delatre Street West

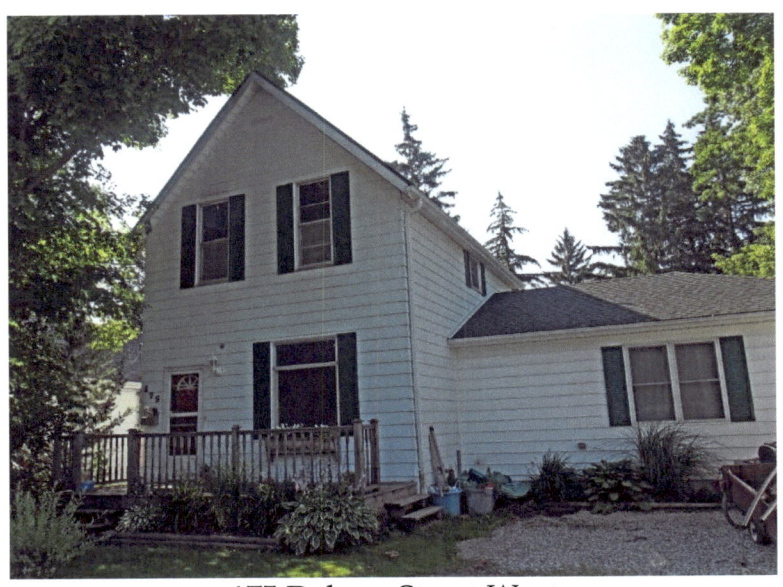

175 Delatre Street West

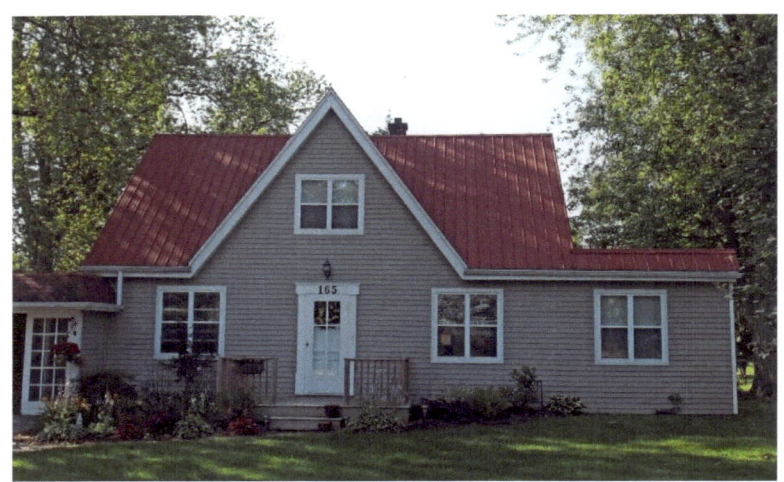

165 Delatre Street West - vernacular

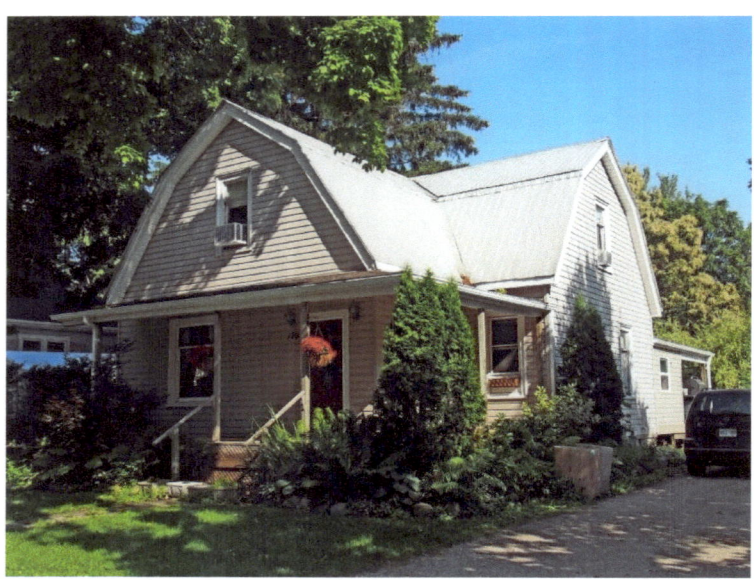

170 Delatre Street West – gambrel roof

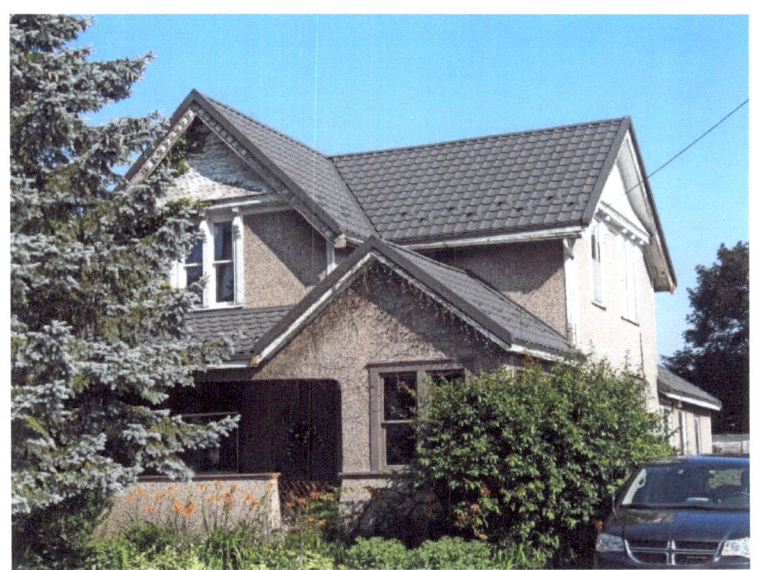

166 Delatre Street West

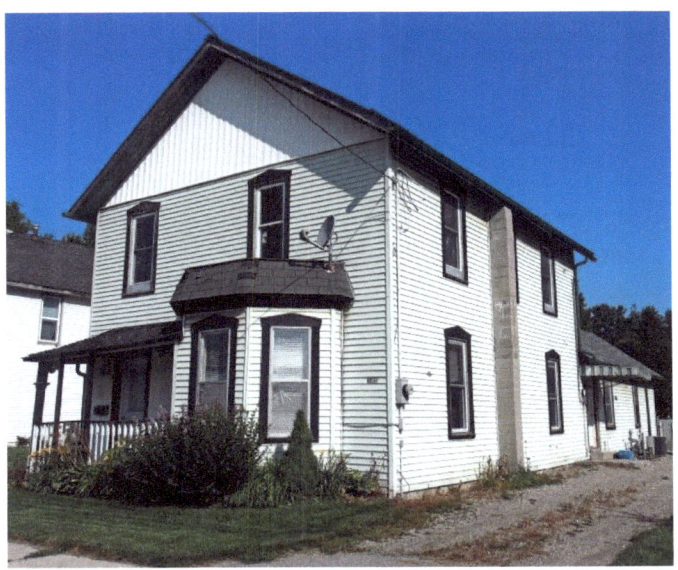

146 Delatre Street West

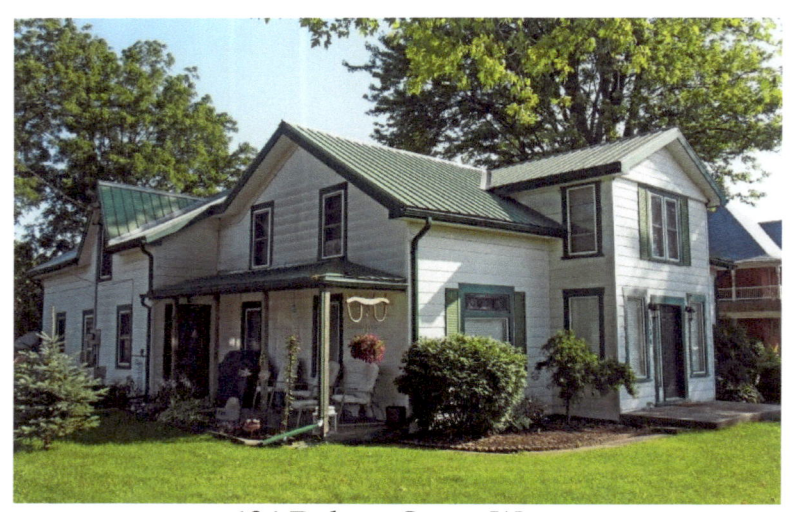

134 Delatre Street West

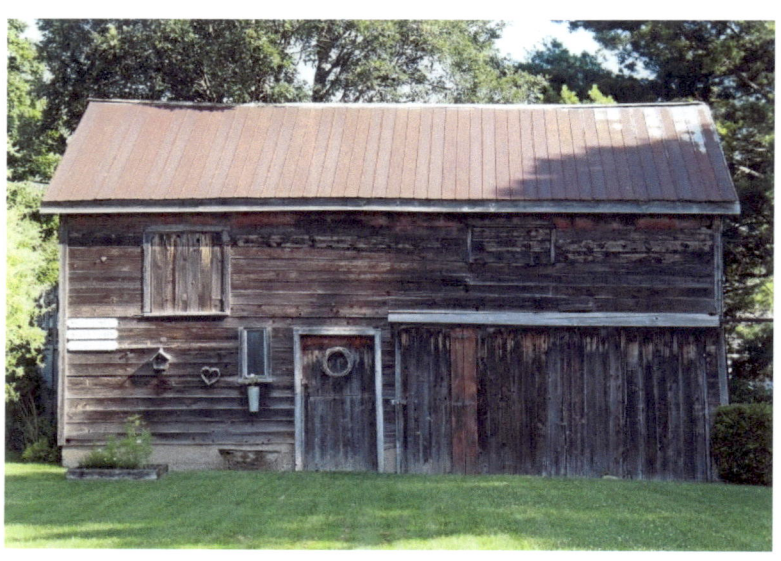

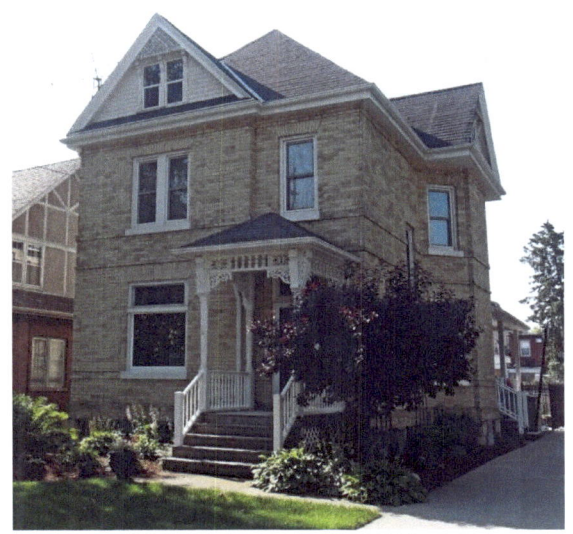

131 Delatre Street West

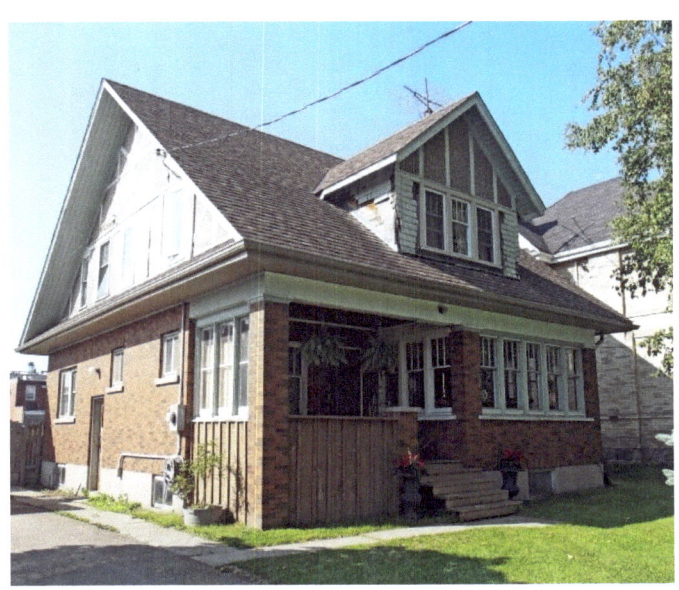

127 Delatre Street West – Tudor half-timbering

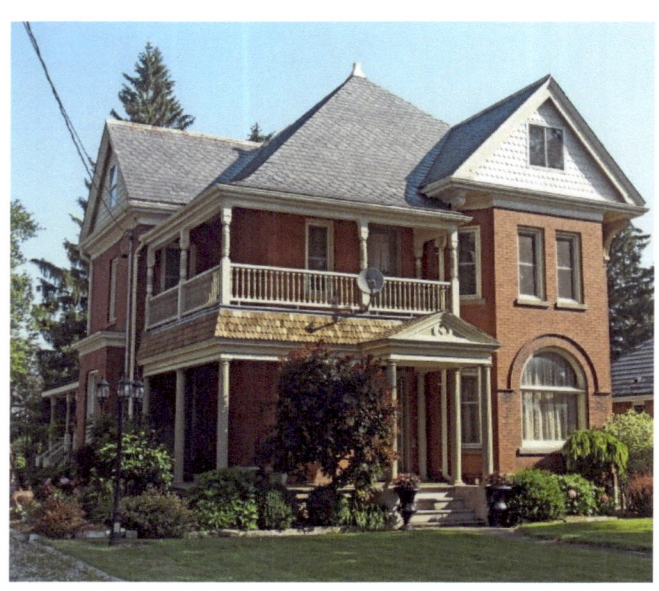

128 Delatre Street West – St. Andrew's Manse 1897
"sleeping porch" on second floor, turned wood spindle
supports, fretwork, pediment with decorated tympanum

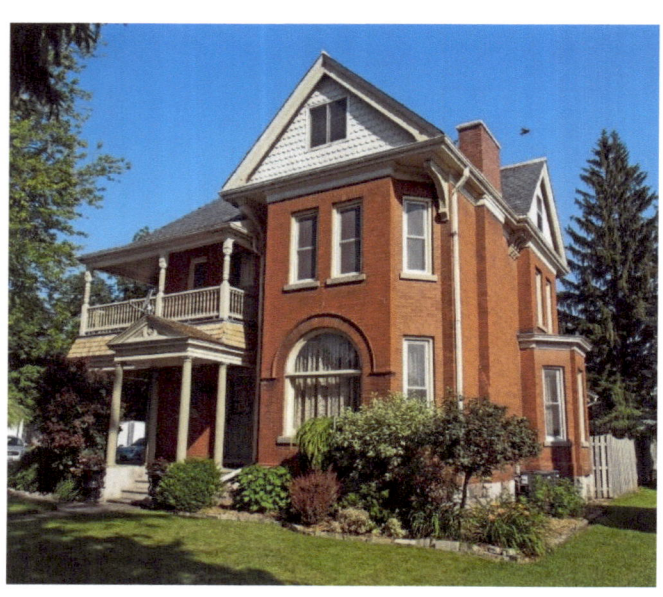

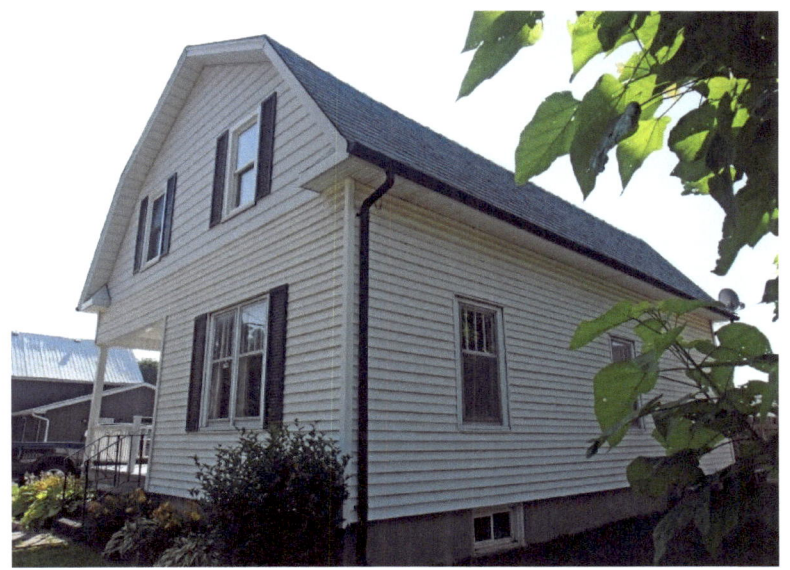

Delatre Street West – gambrel roof

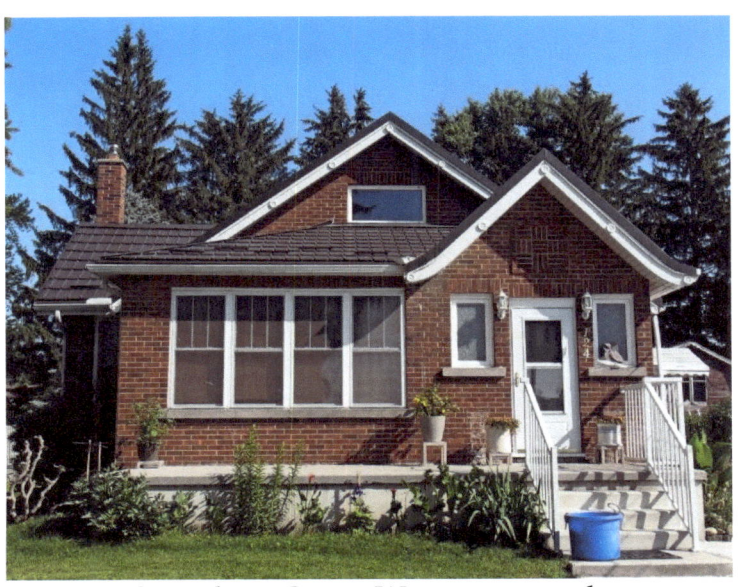

124 Delatre Street West - vernacular

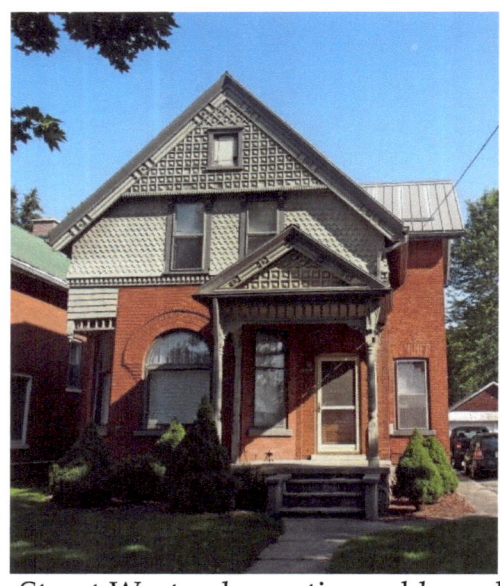

118 Delatre Street West – decorative gable and pediment, Romanesque style window voussoir

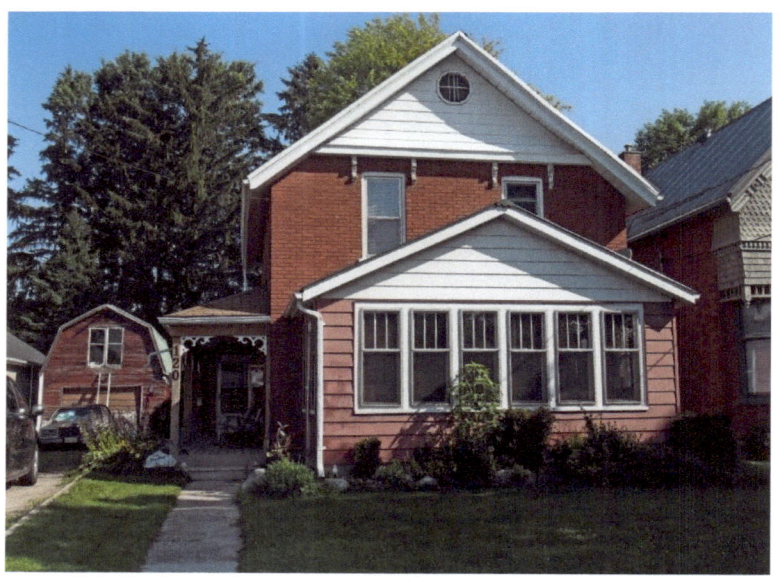

120 Delatre Street West – bric-a-brac on porch, single cornice brackets

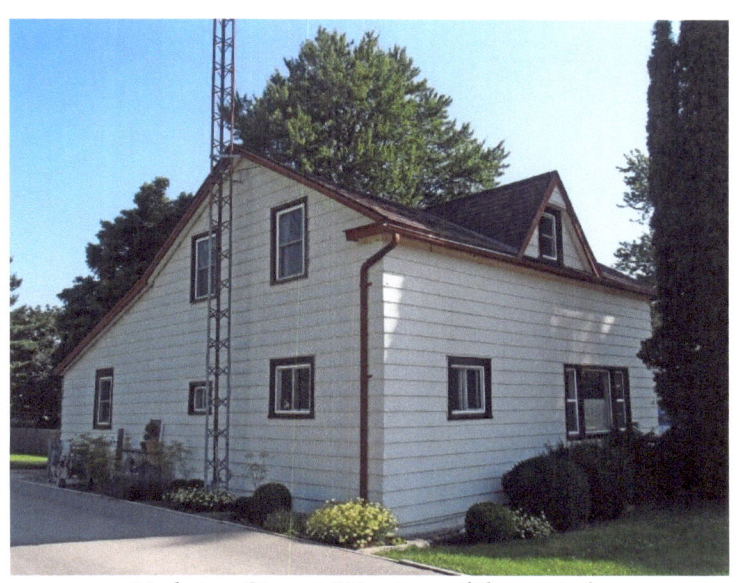

Delatre Street West – saltbox style

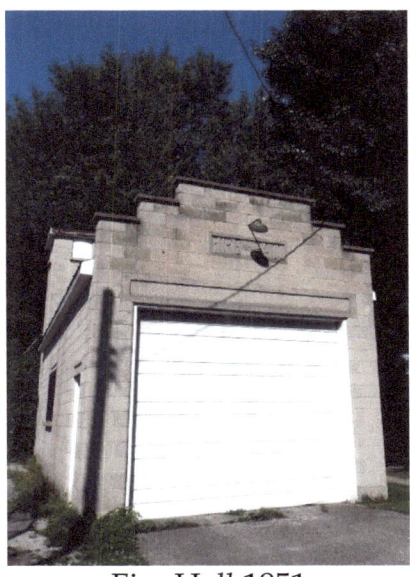

Fire Hall 1951

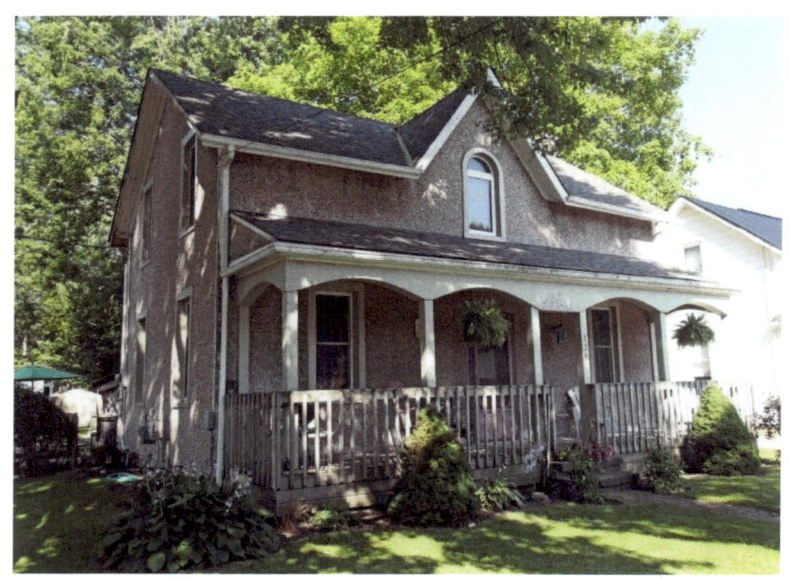

135 George Street – Gothic Revival

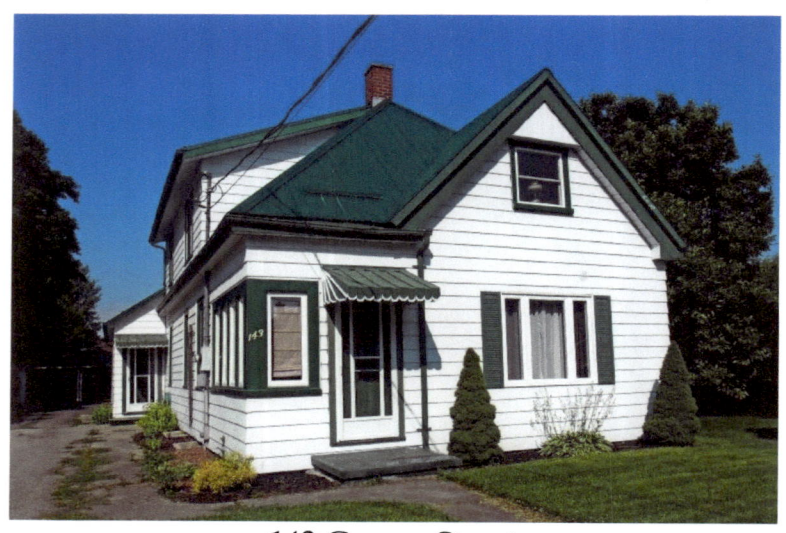

143 George Street

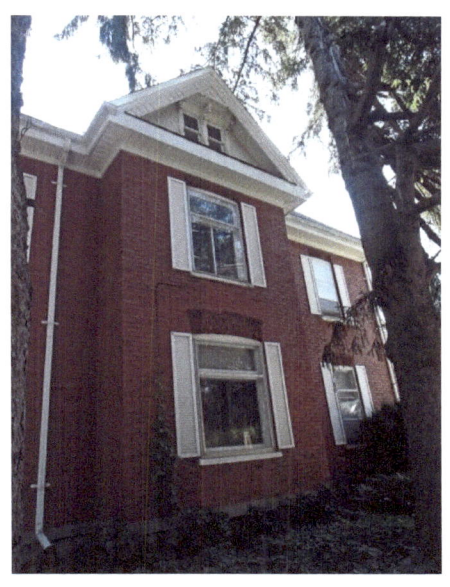

George Street – Edwardian, decorative gable, semi-circular
stained glass window topped by voussoir

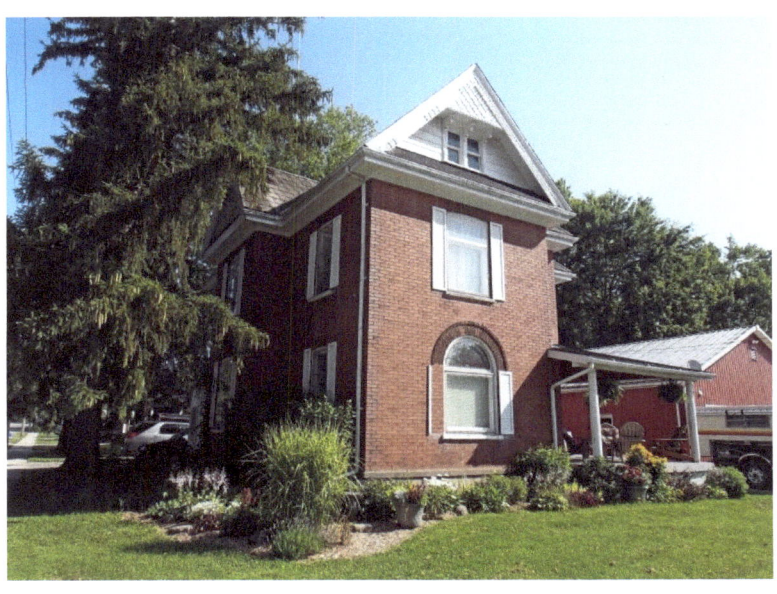

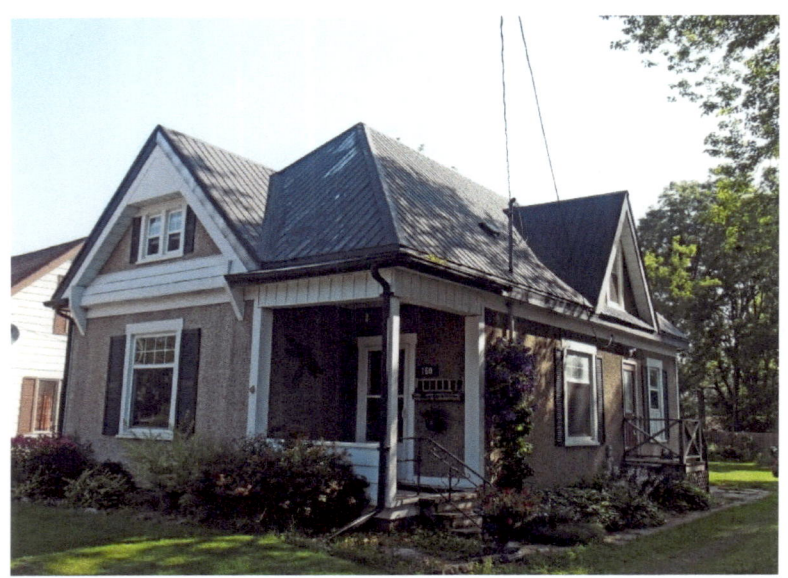

150 George Street - vernacular

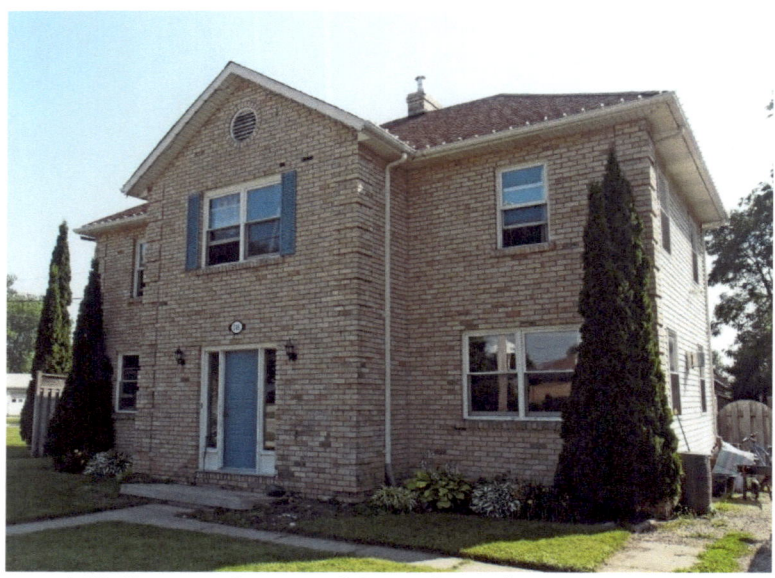

168 George Street – hipped roof, corner quoins

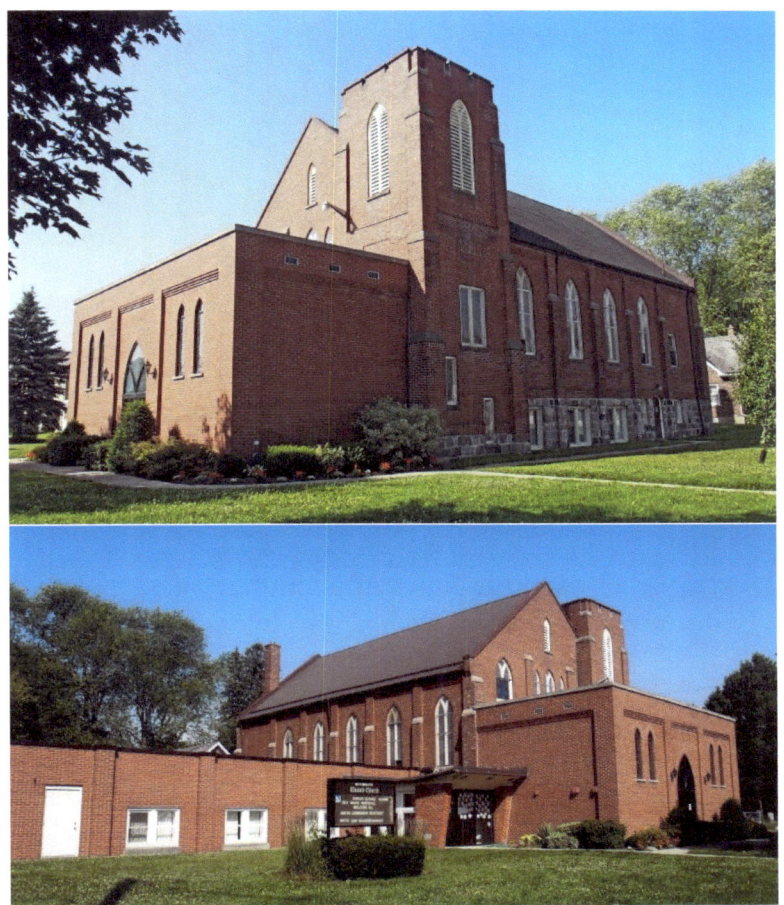

115 George Street – Westminster United Church - The Scottish Presbyterians who settled here constructed a small frame building in 1847. In later years, a magnificent stone structure was erected with a tower and lovely stained glass windows. Gaelic services were held as a second service. Wesley Methodist Church was established in 1854. The two congregations united in 1927 to form the Thamesford United Church. In 1938, Westminster United Church was built and dedicated. - Gothic Revival style - lancet windows, buttresses, cobblestone foundation

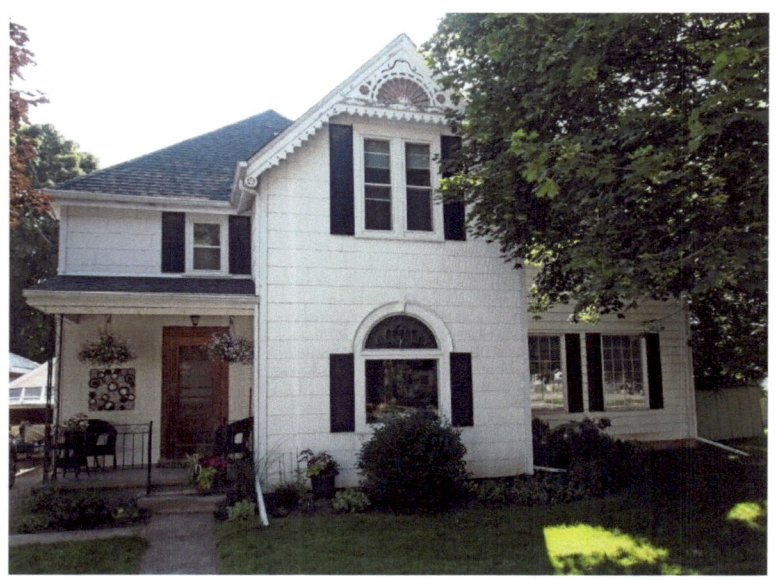

George Street – Gothic Revival - within peak of gable is a
decorative arch with applied scrollwork, spindles
and circular piercing

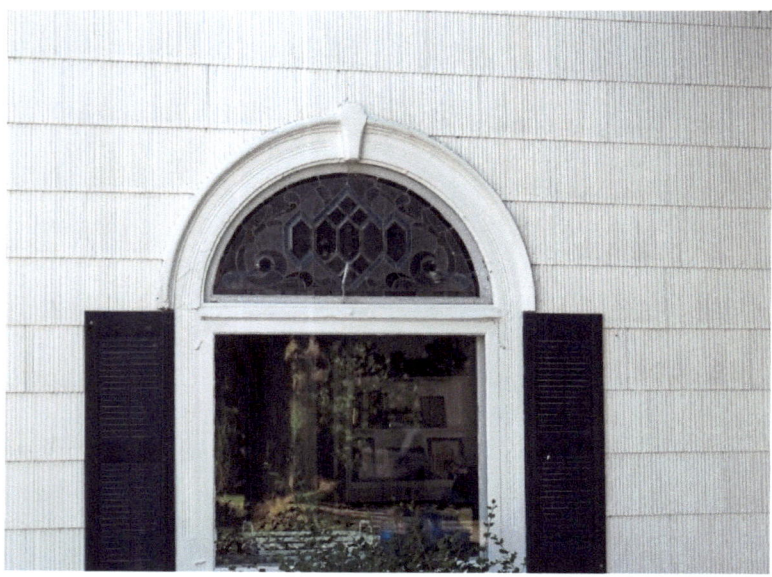

Stained glass window, drip moulding with keystone

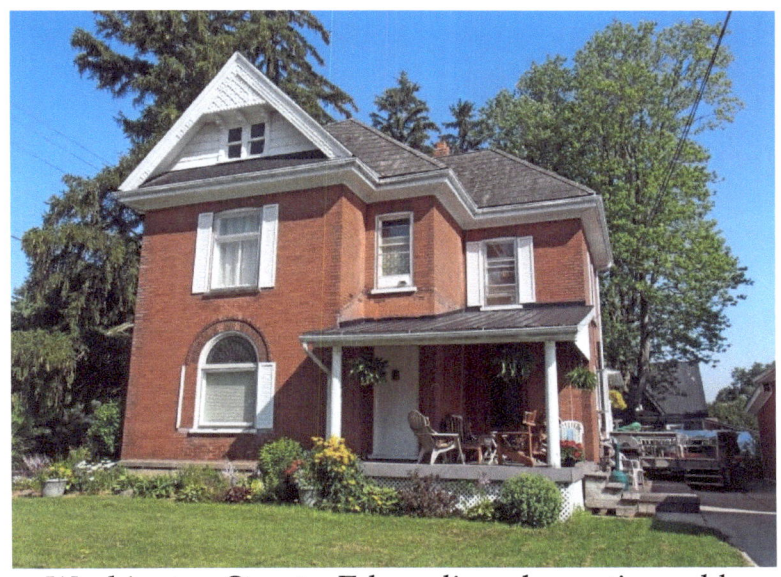

Washington Street – Edwardian, decorative gable

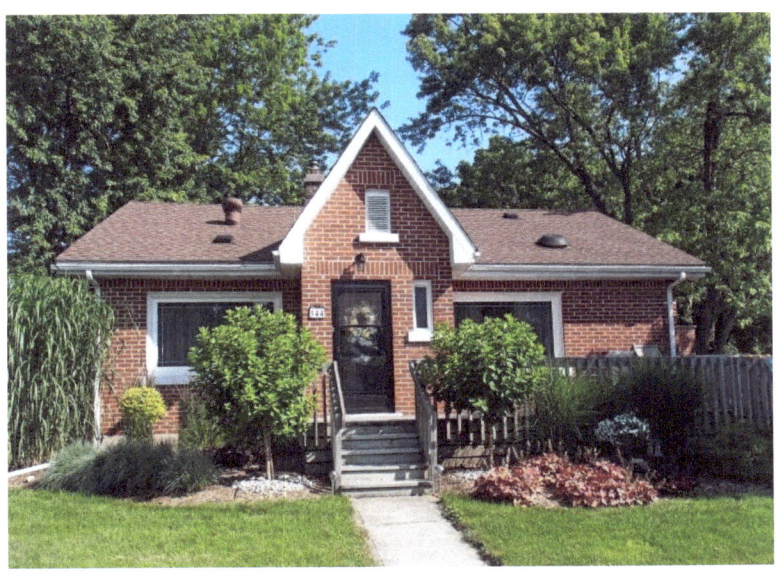

144 Washington Street – Regency cottage

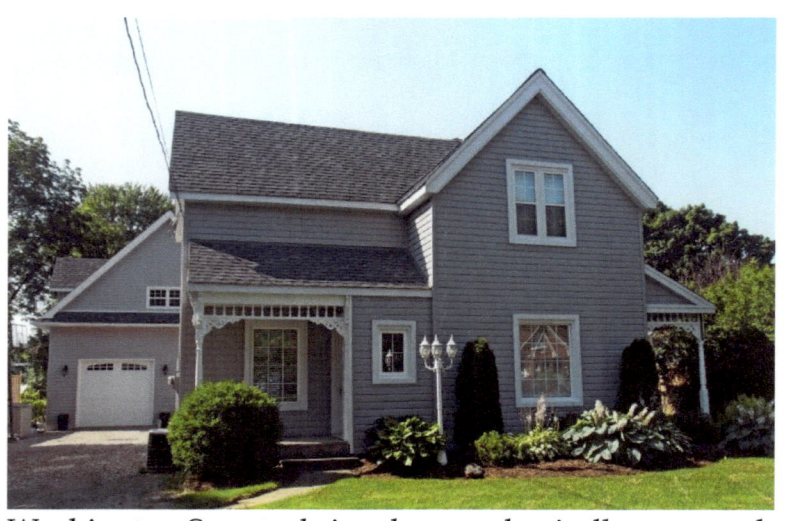

Washington Street – bric-a-brac and spindles on porch

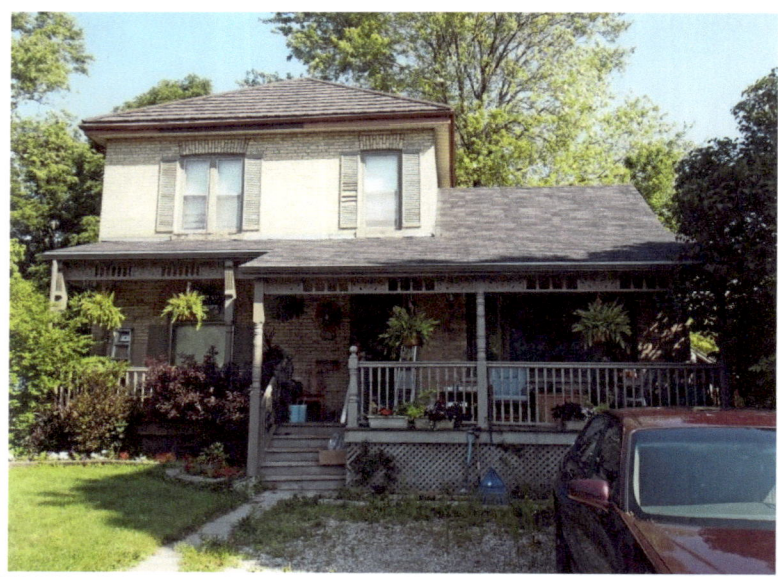

138 Washington Street – spindles and stenciling on porch,
turned wooden supports

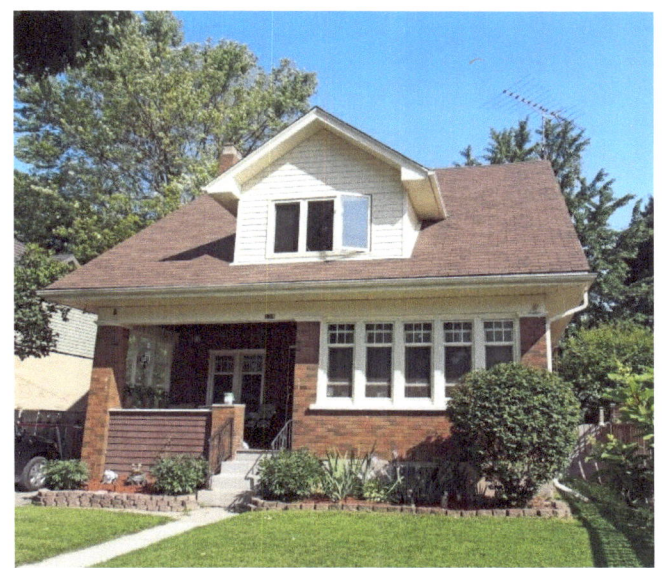

134 Washington Street – dormer in attic

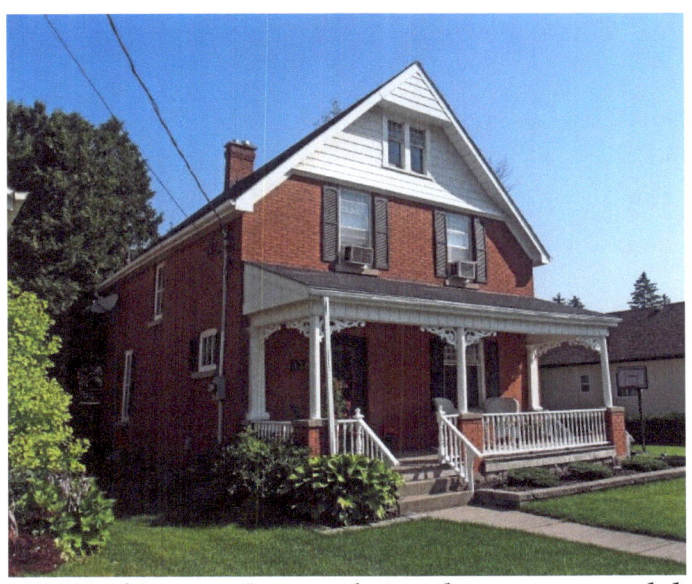

128 Washington Street – bric-a-brac on verandah

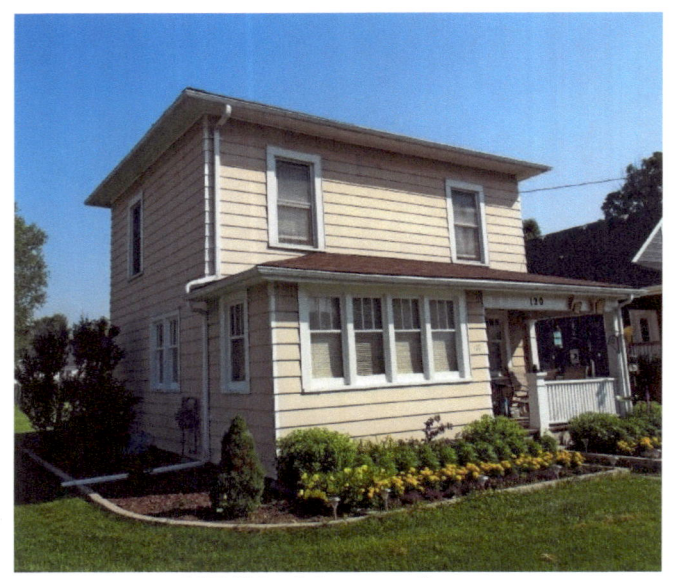

120 Washington Street

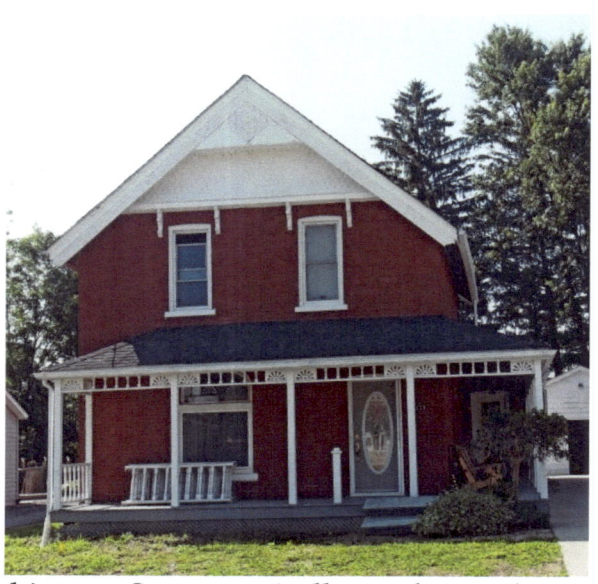

121 Washington Street – spindles and stenciling on porch

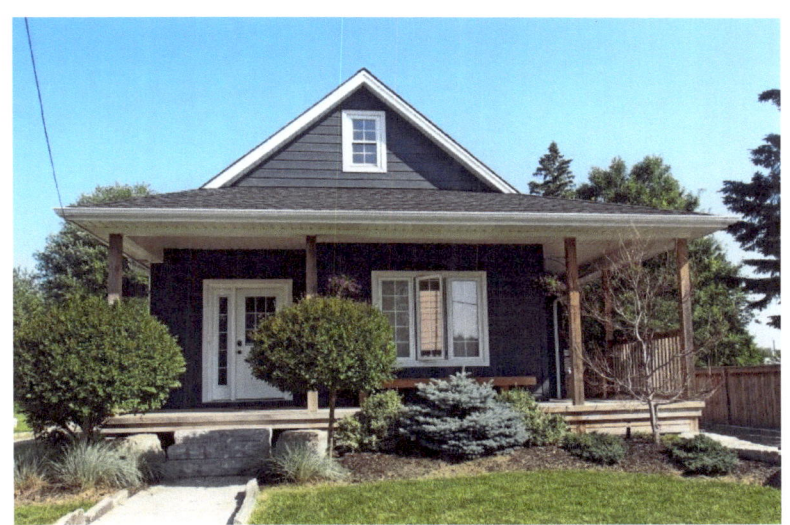

Washington Street

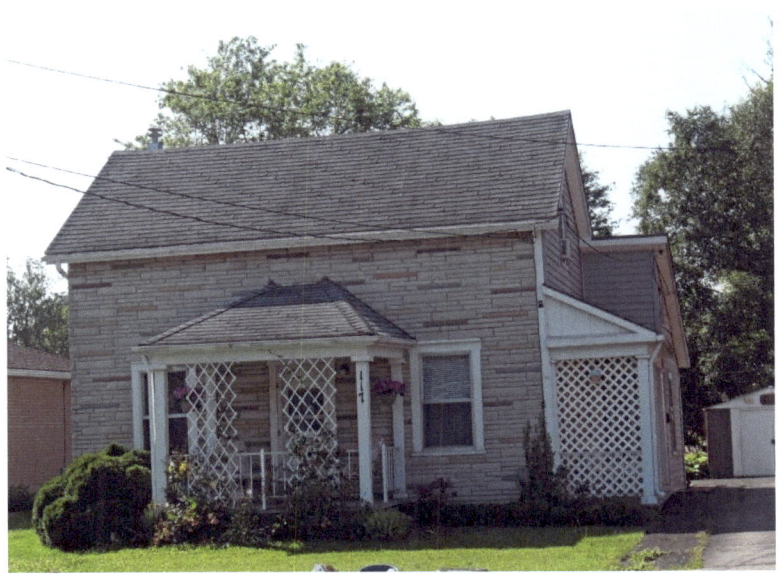

117 Washington Street

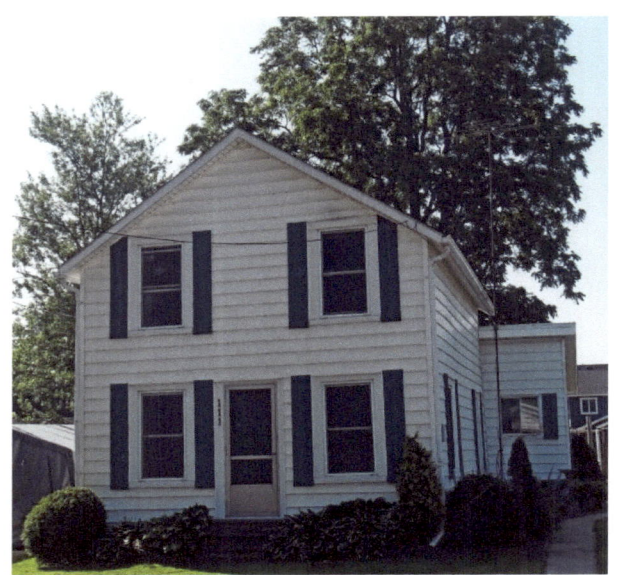

111 Washington Street

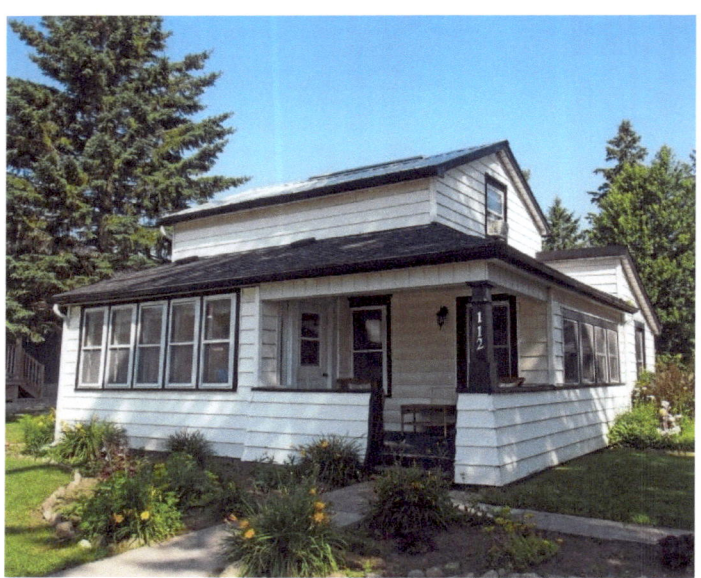

112 Washington Street

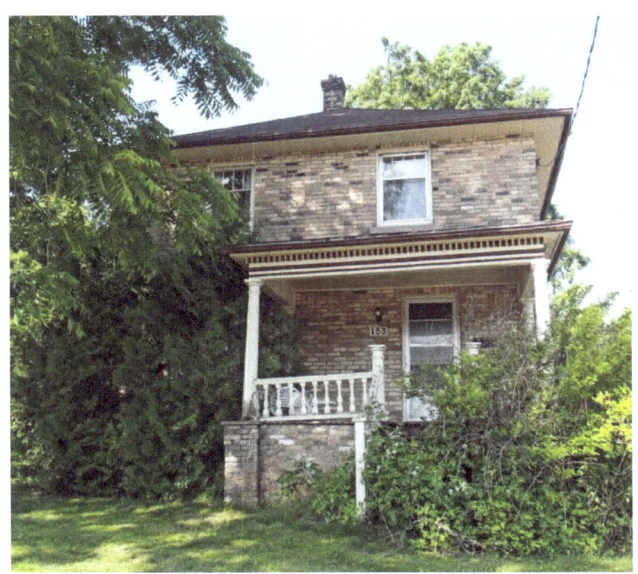

153 Allen Street – Italianate, hipped roof

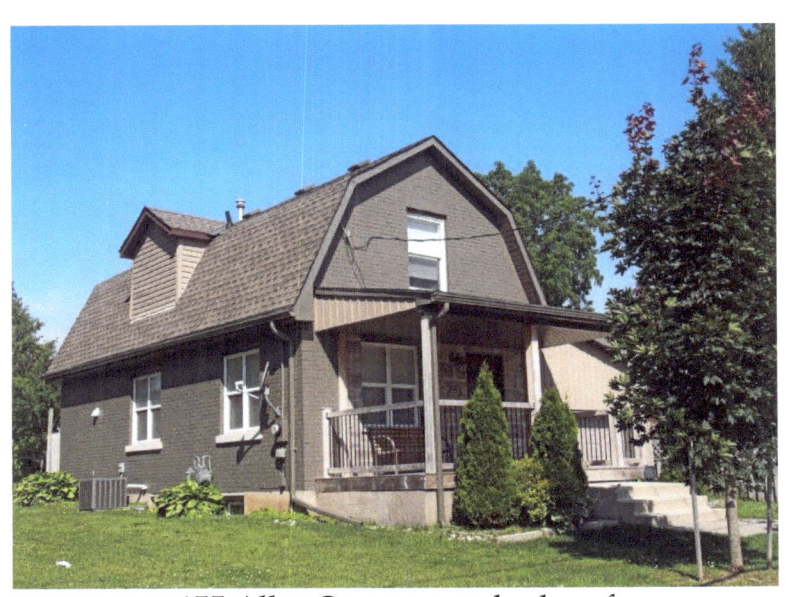

155 Allen Street – gambrel roof

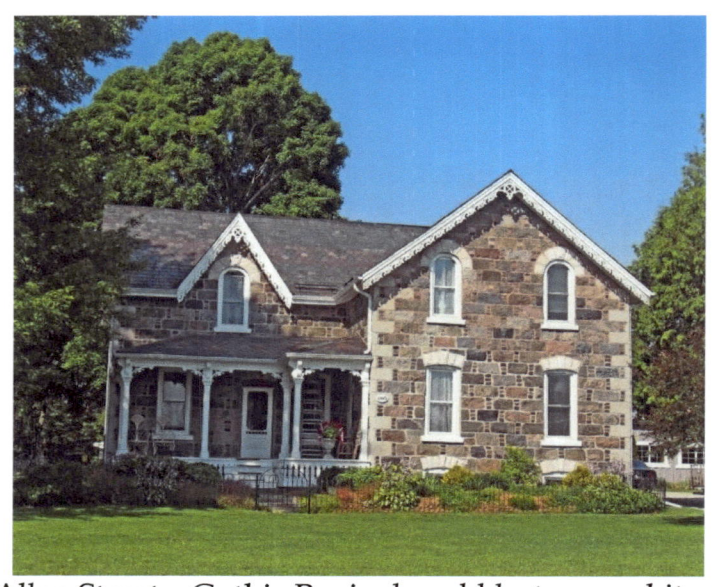

205 Allen Street – Gothic Revival - cobblestone architecture, corner quoins

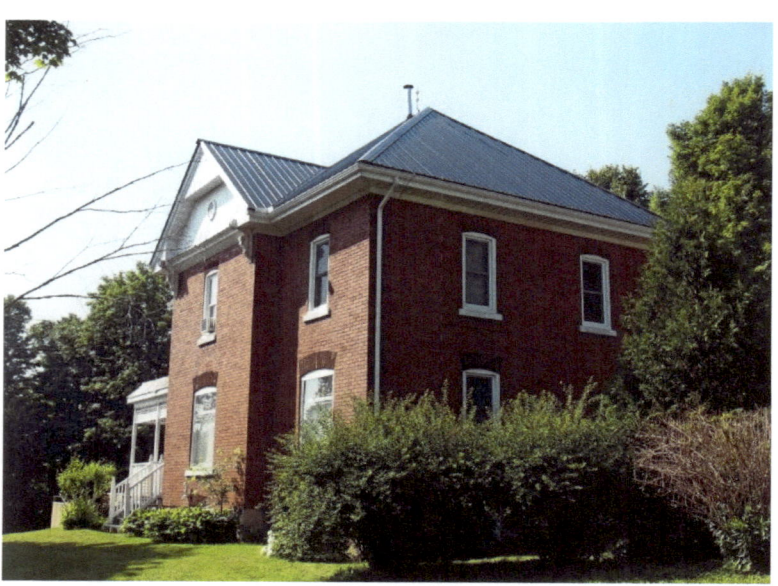

Allen Street – Italianate – hipped roof

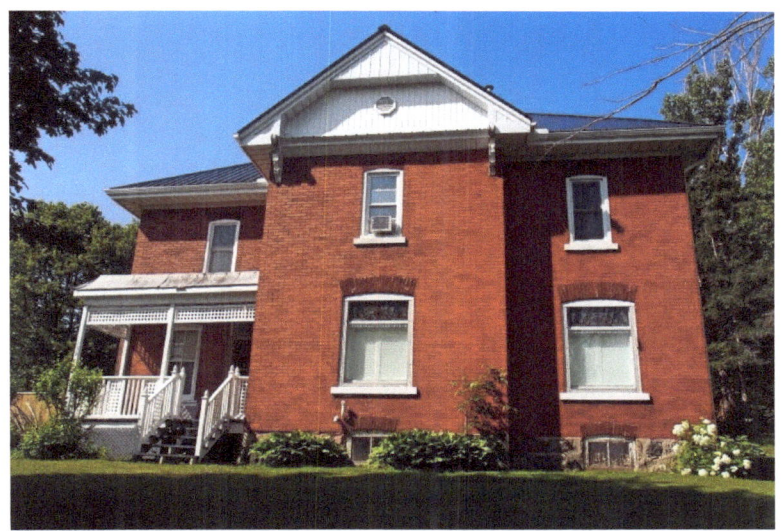

Allen Street – hipped roof with two-storey tower-like bay topped with pediment

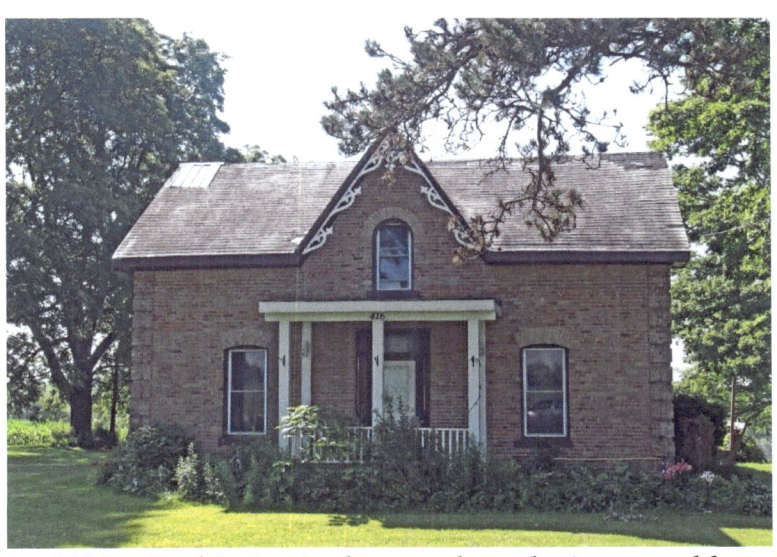

#416 – Gothic Revival, verge board trim on gable

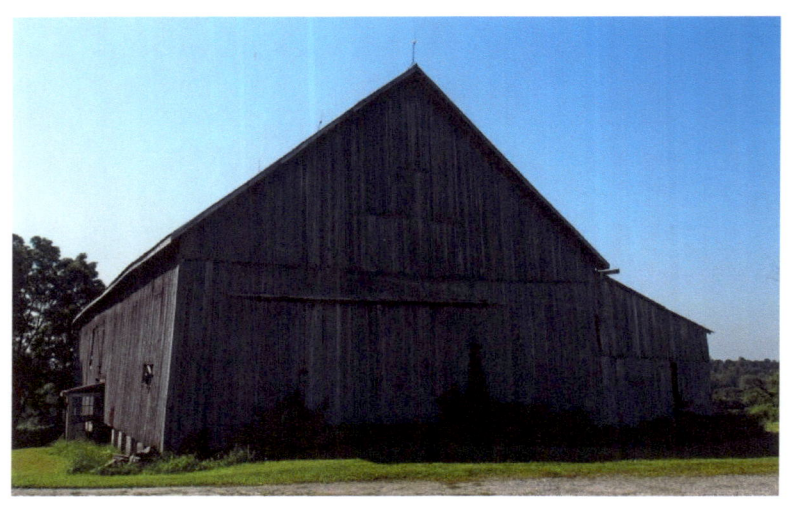

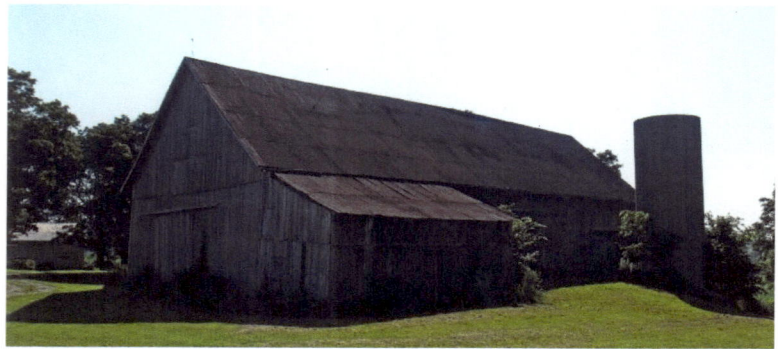

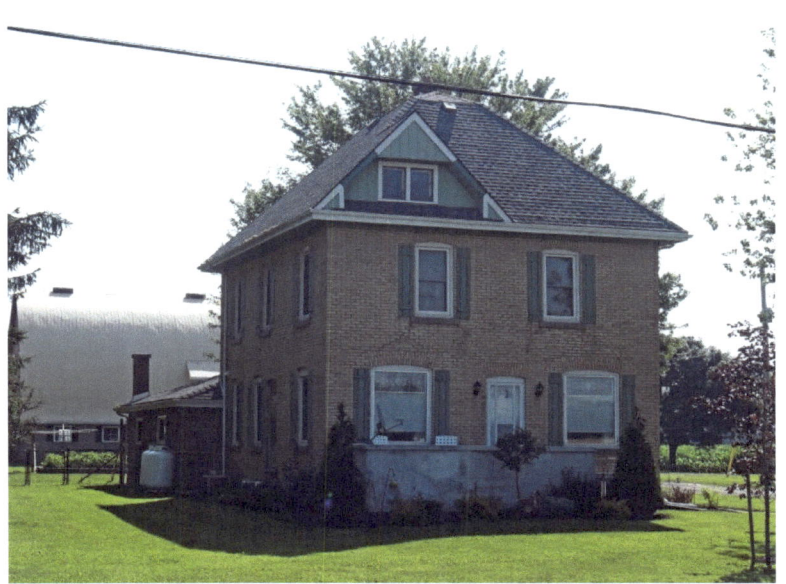

Steeply pitched hipped roof, full two-storeys

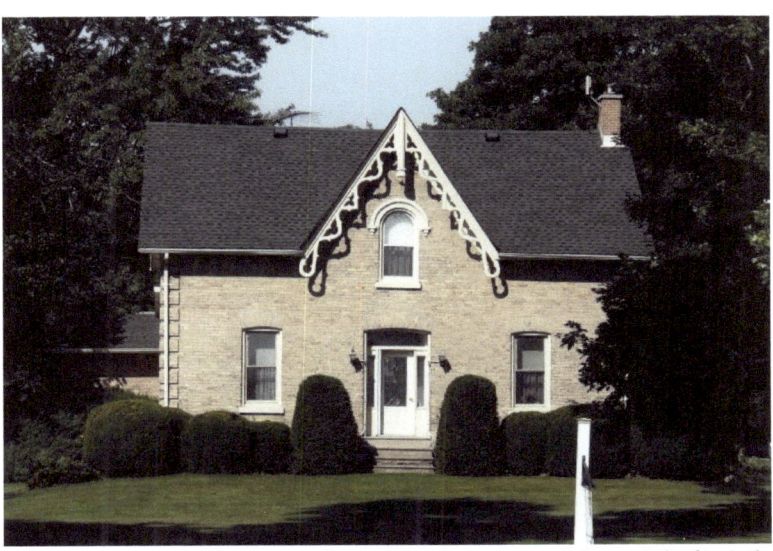

Gothic Revival, verge board trim on gable with finial

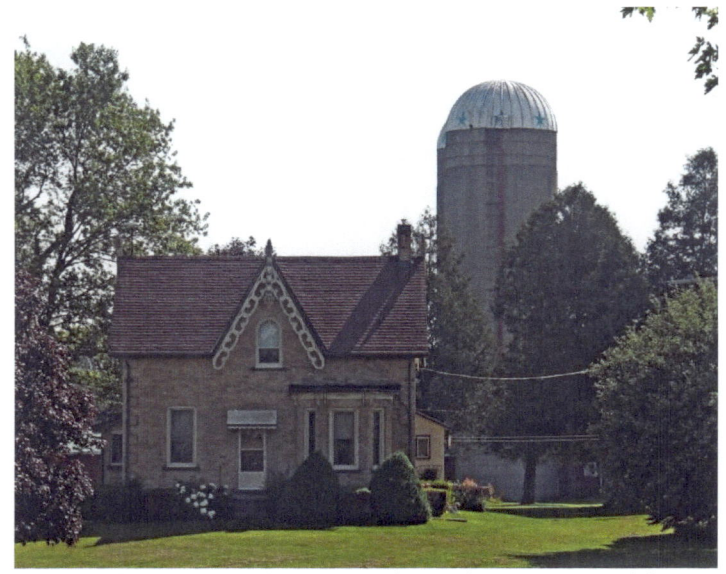

Gothic Revival – verge board trim on gable

Putnam

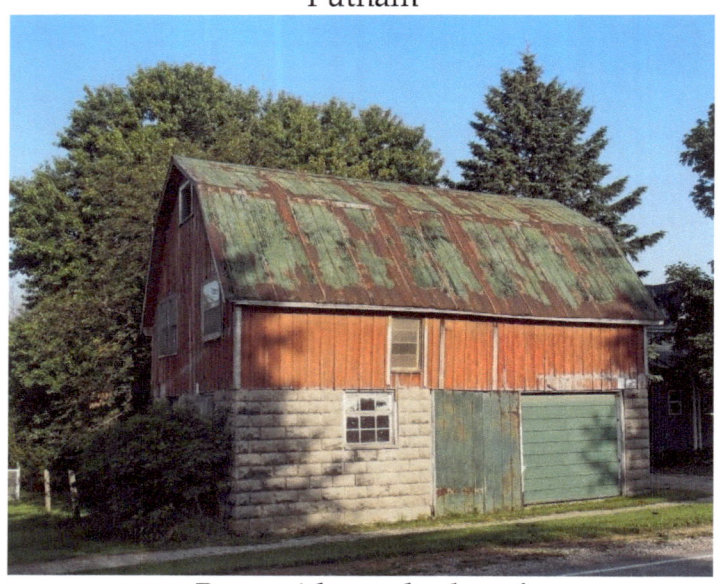

Barn with gambrel roof

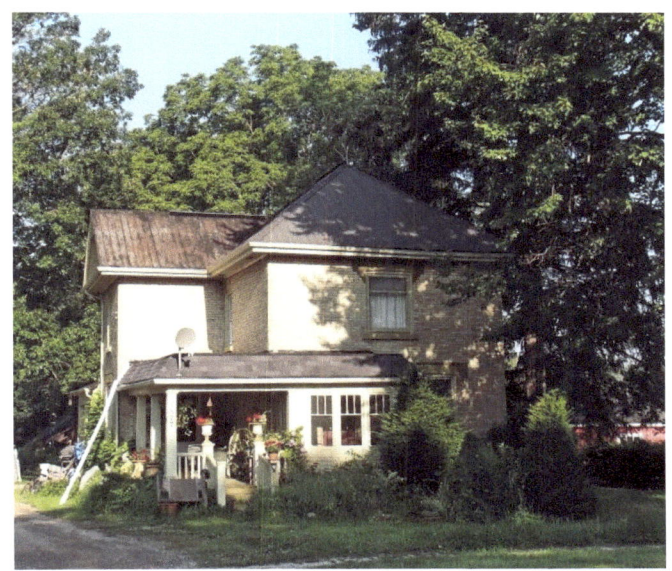

#2877

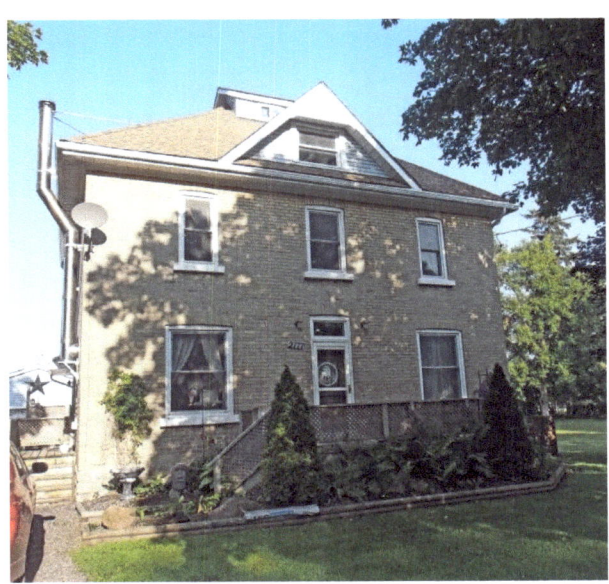

#2777 – full two-storeys

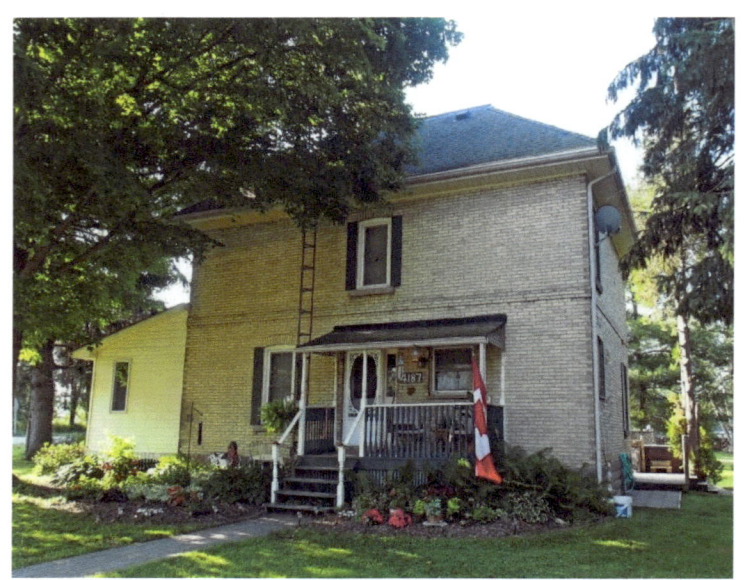

#4187 – hipped roof

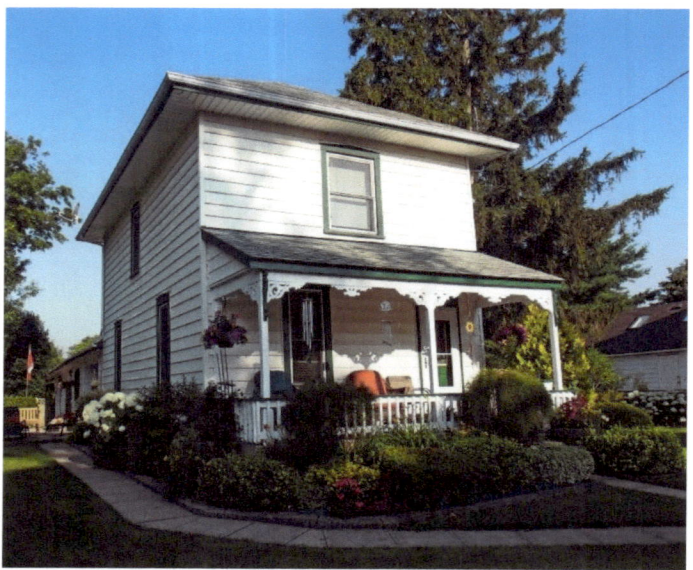

Hipped roof, bric-a-brac on verandah

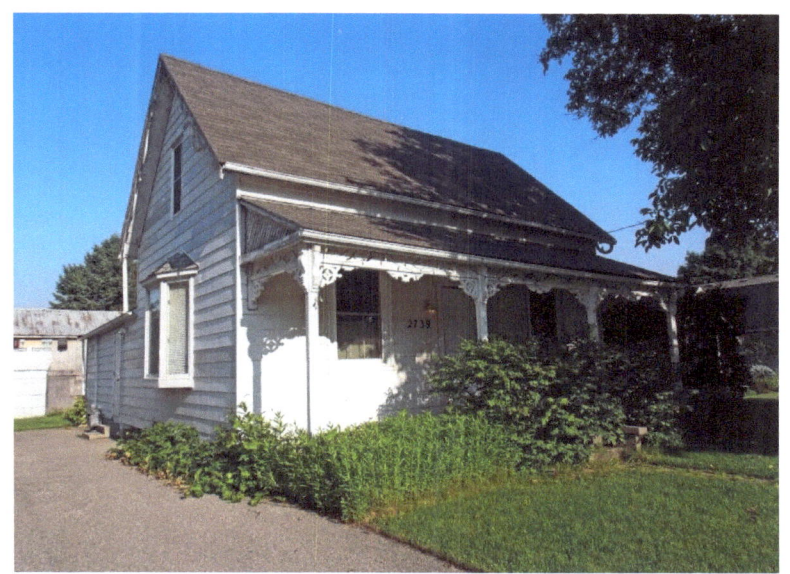

#2739 - bric-a-brac on verandah

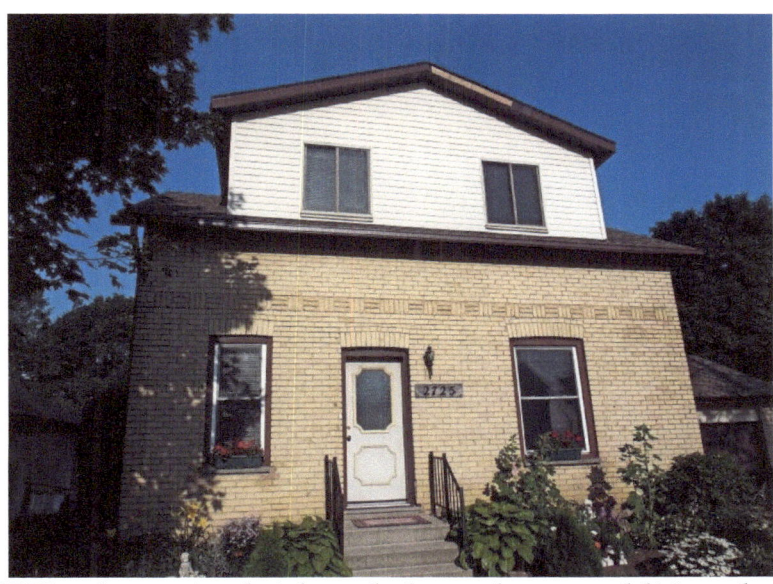

#2725 – decorative brickwork; large dormer addition above roof

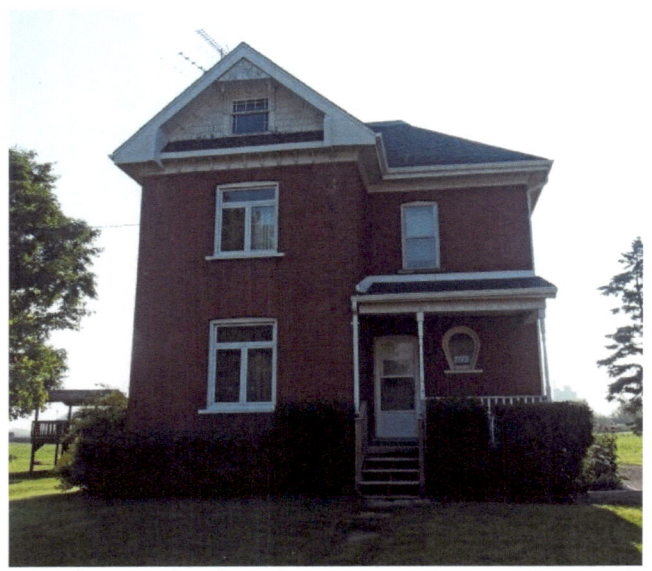

#2722 – single cornice brackets, turned verandah roof supports

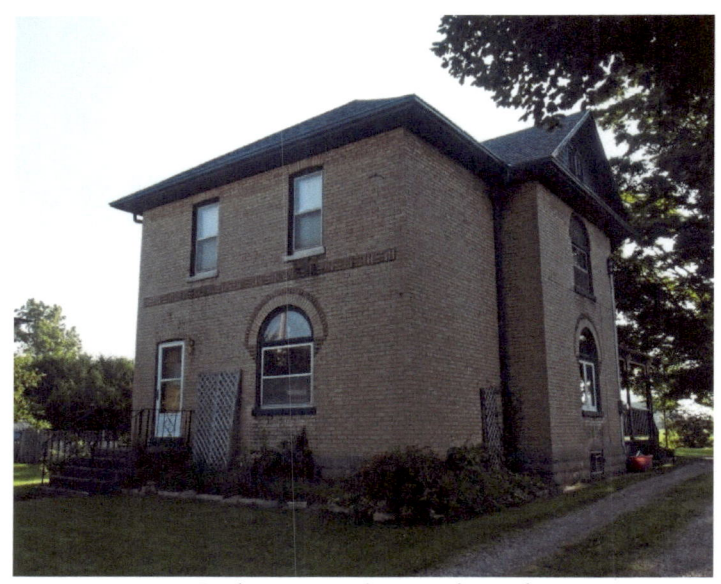

Italianate – hipped roof

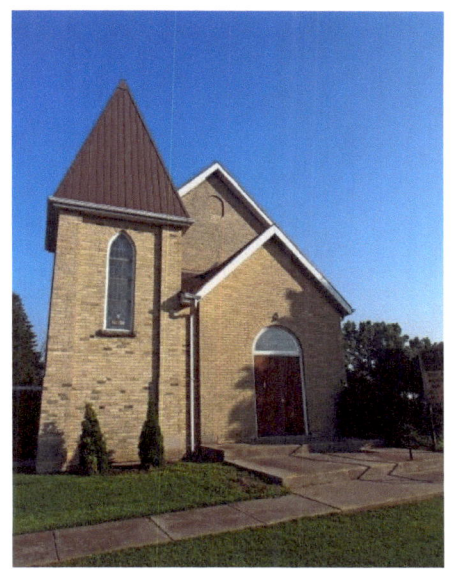

Putnam United Church – lancet window

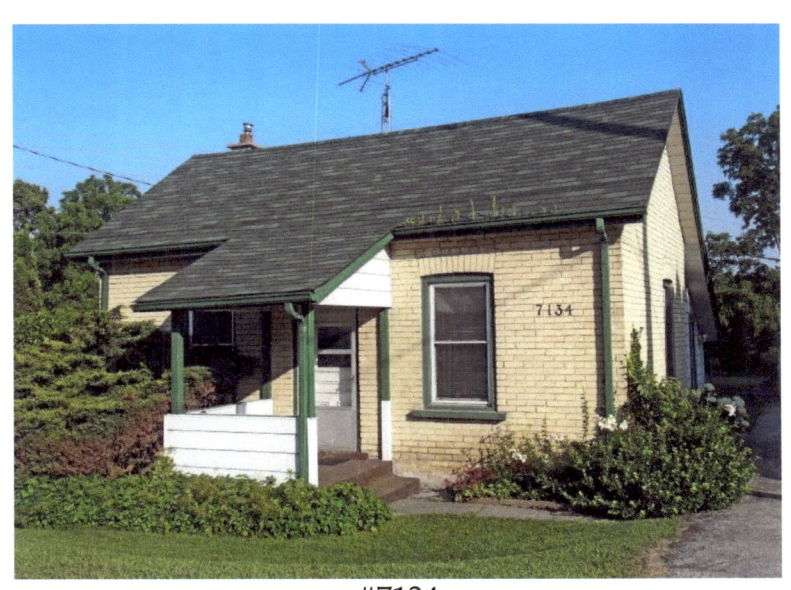

#7134

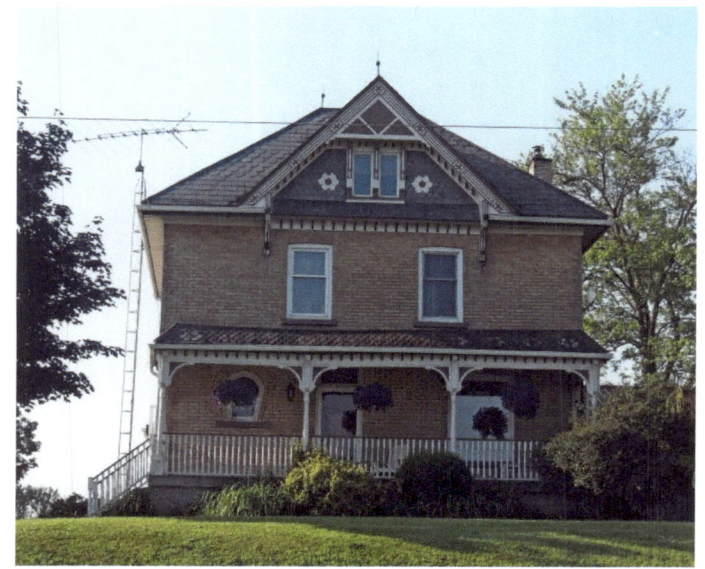

Turned verandah roof supports, decorative gable, verge board trim, fish scale pattern, cornice brackets

Kintore

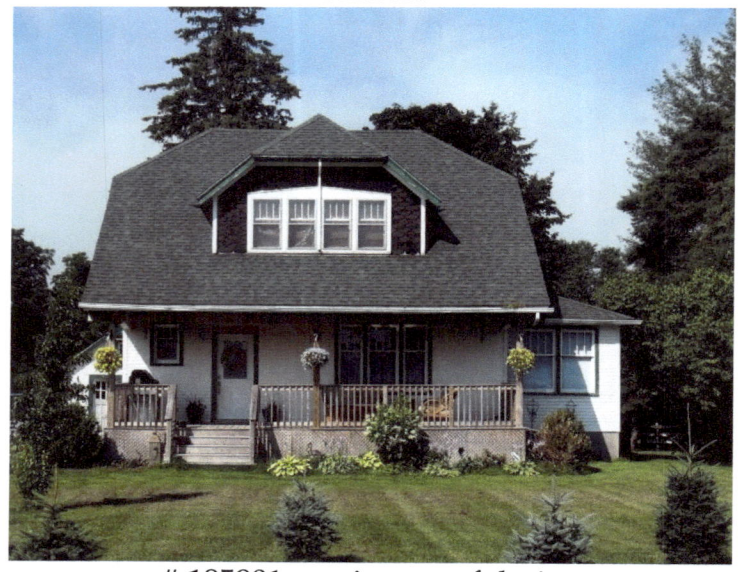

195901 – unique roof design

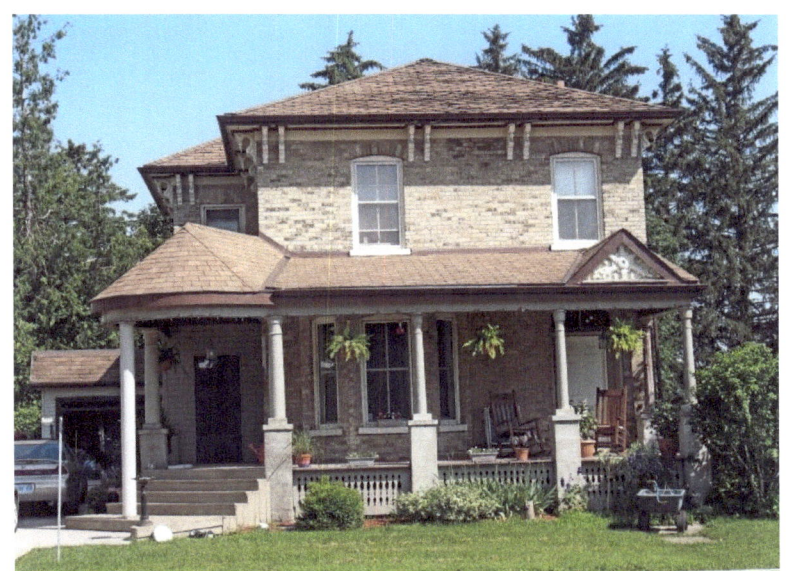

Italianate – hipped roof, paired cornice brackets, pediment
with decorated tympanum

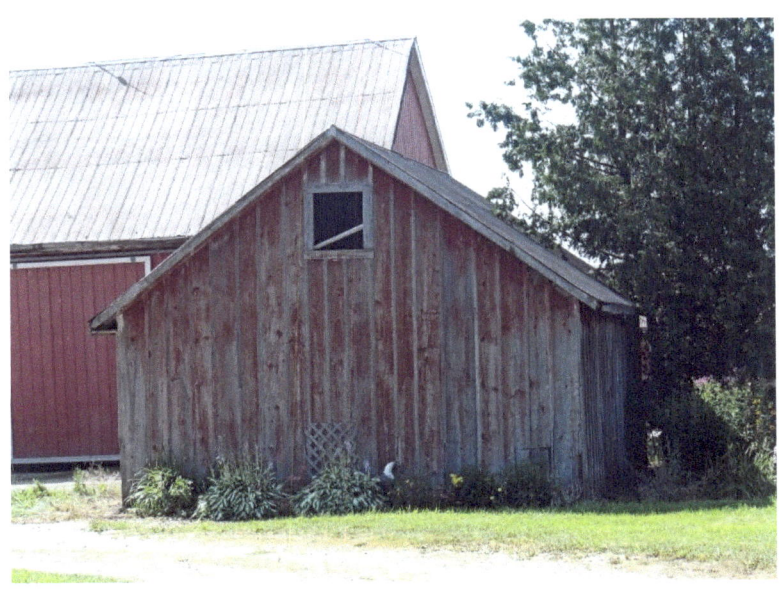

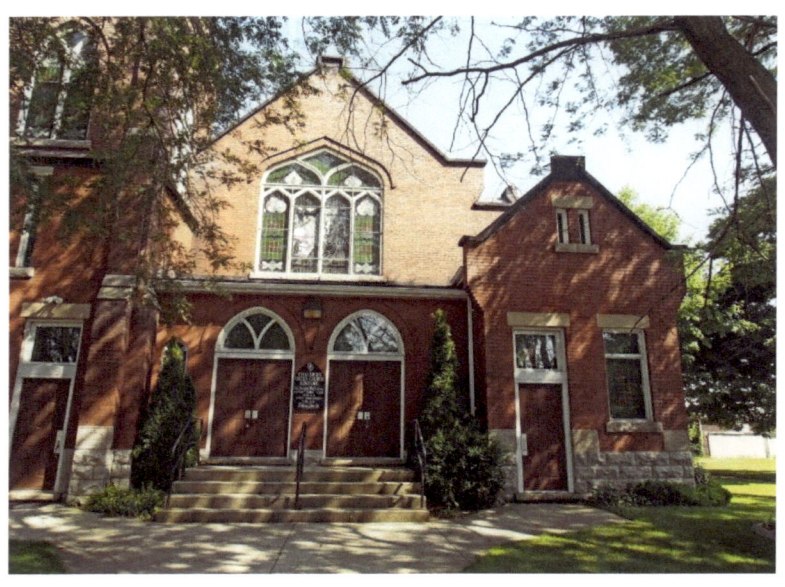

842989 Road 84, Kintore - Chalmers United Church, Kintore
This church is the result of the union of Trinity United Church
and Chalmers Presbyterian Church in 1927.
It was built in 1914.

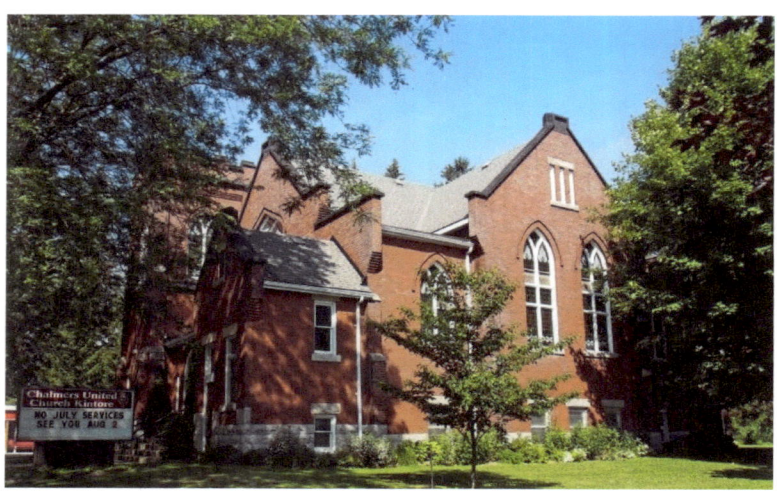

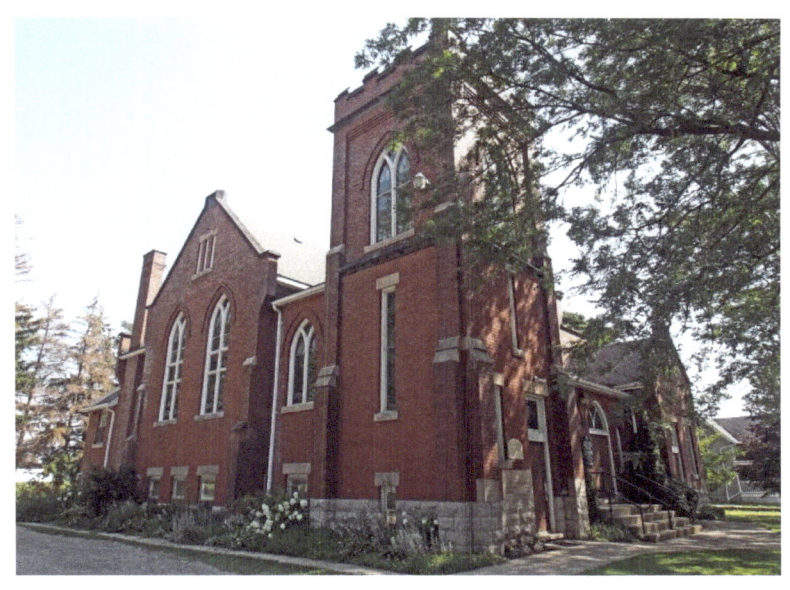

Presbyterian Church – Chalmers United Church, Kintore
A.D. 1871, rebuilt 1914

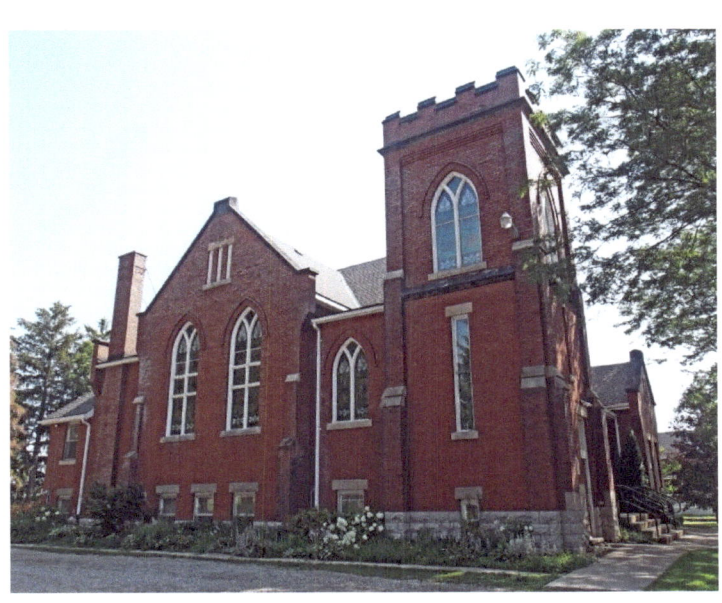

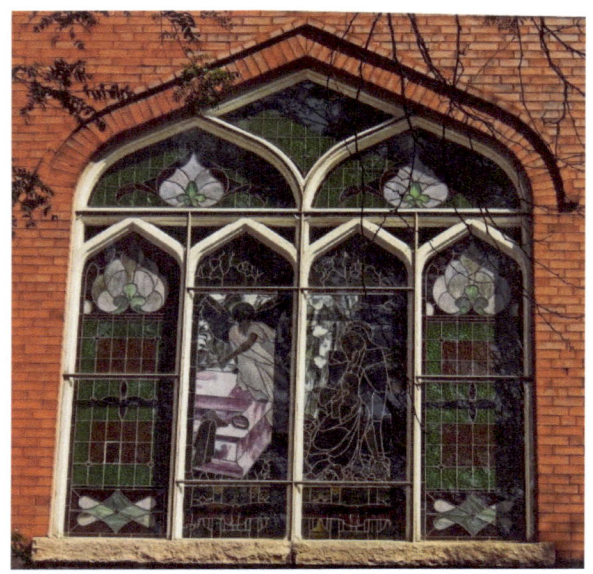

Stained glass window

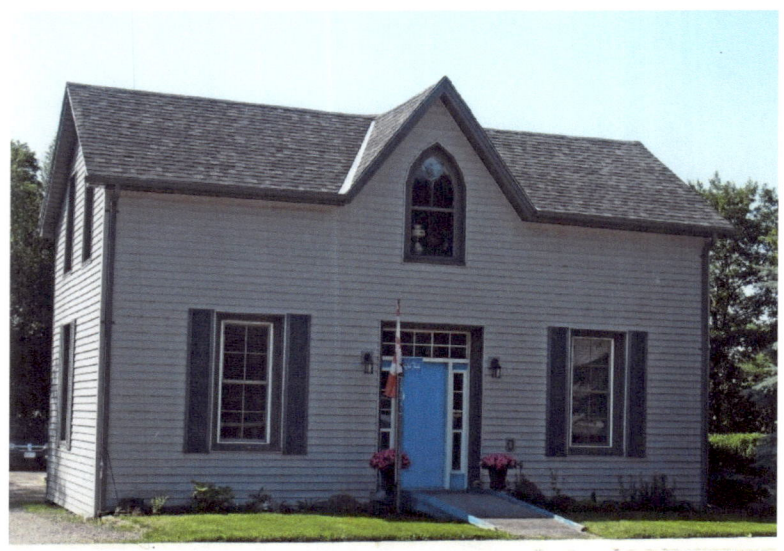

#157 - Gothic

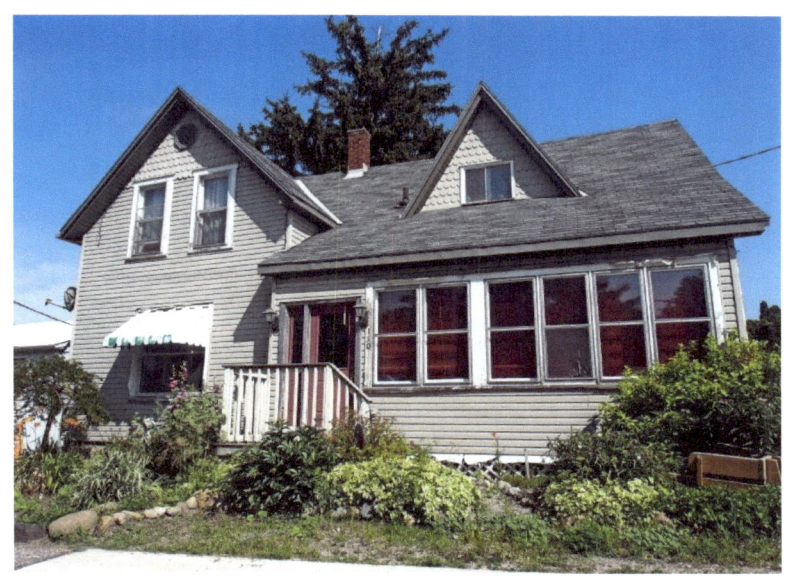

#150 - Gothic

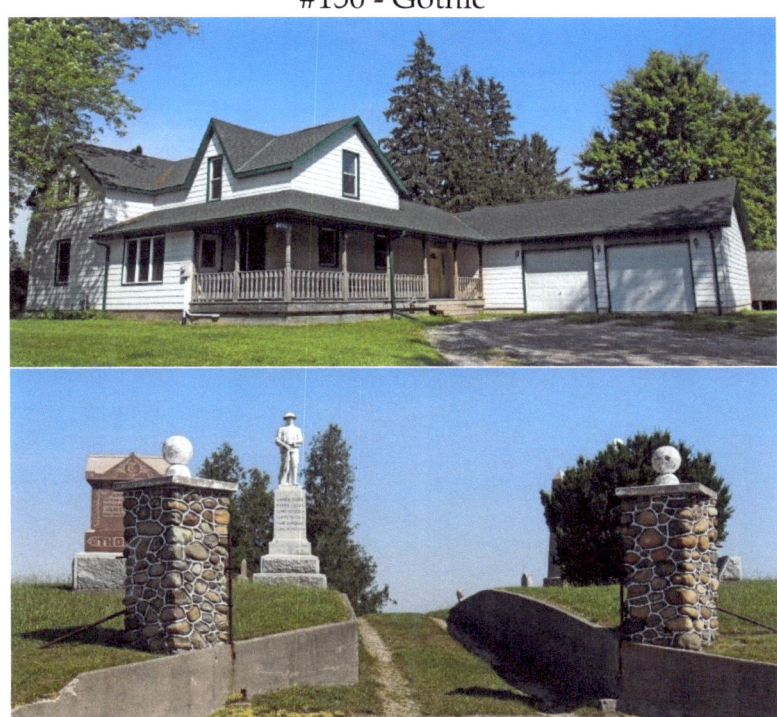

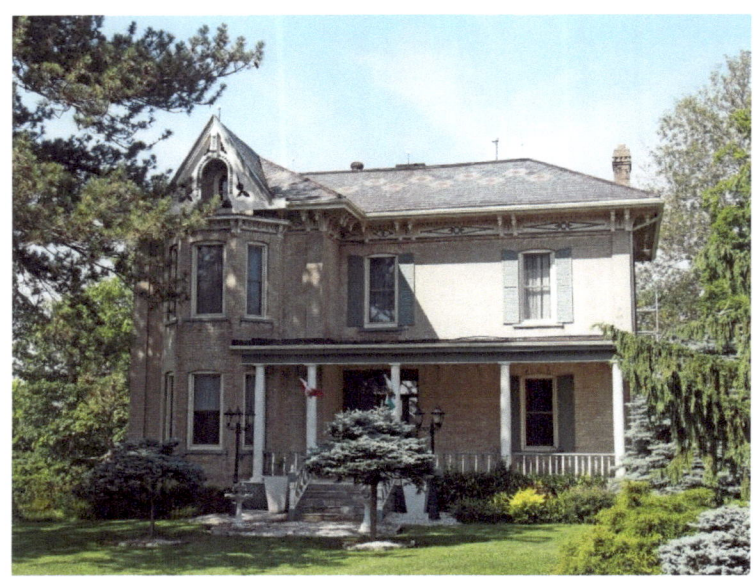

Italianate, hipped roof, cornice brackets, verge board trim on gable, decorative cornice with dentil moulding, two and a half storey tower-like bay, Doric pillars supporting the verandah, trichromatic tile work on the roof

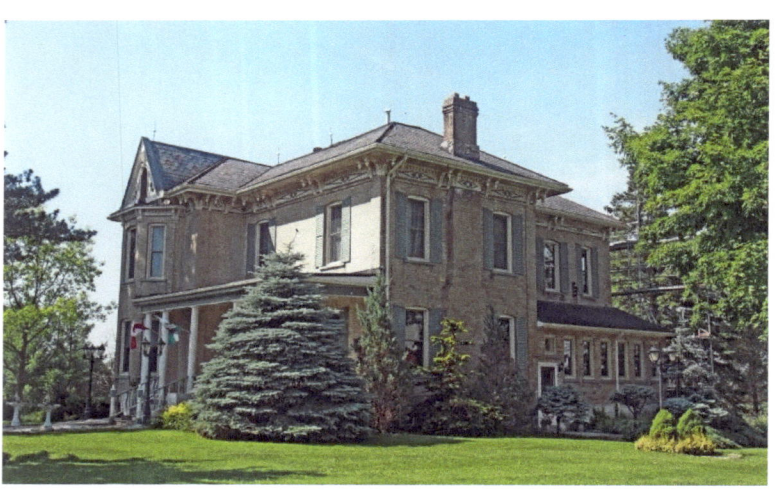

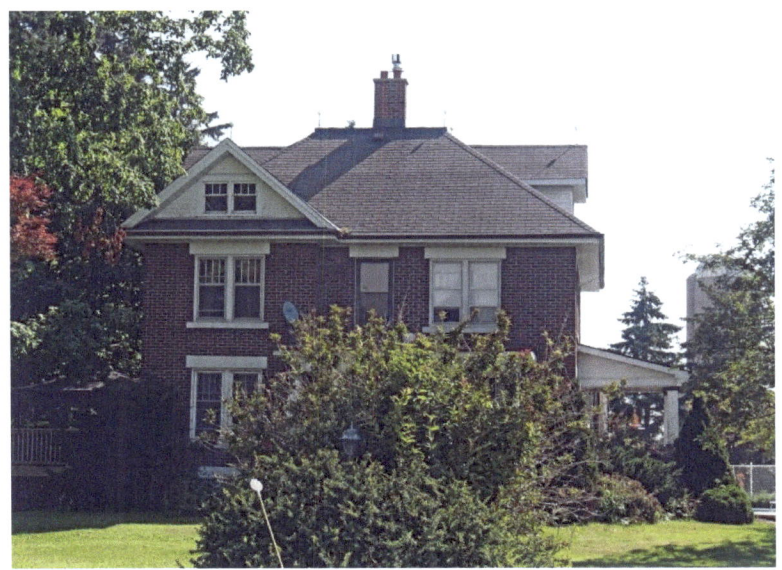

Edwardian

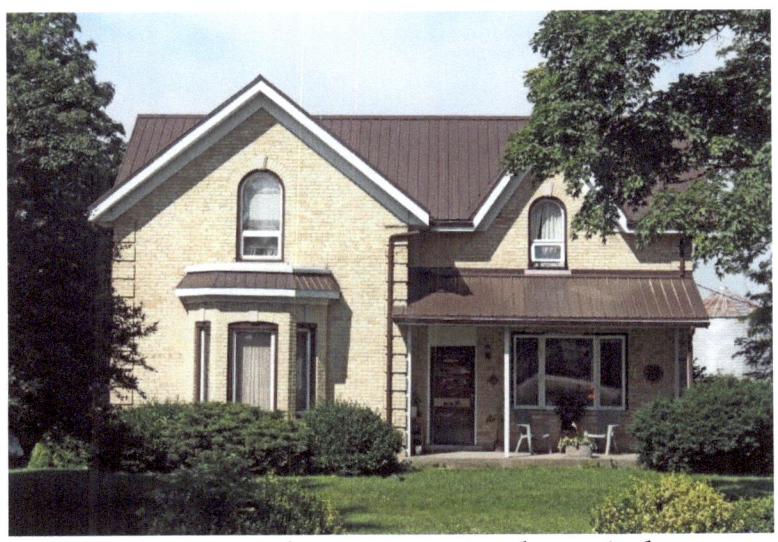

Gothic Revival, corner quoins, bay window

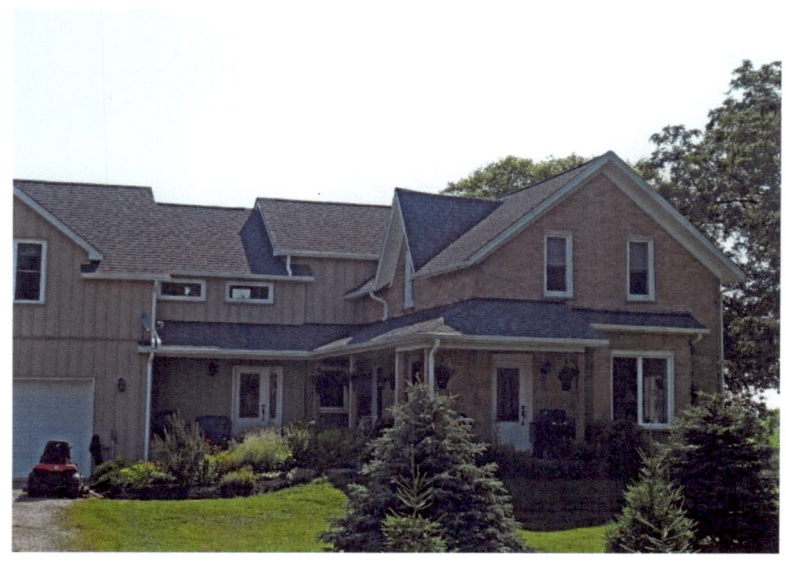

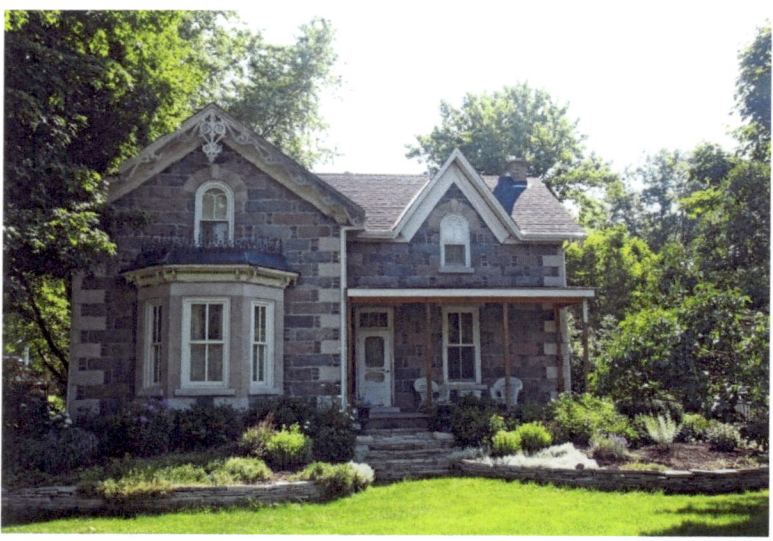

Gothic Revival – cobblestone architecture, bay window with iron cresting above, corner quoins, verge board trim on gable with finial, voussoirs with keystones, transom window above door

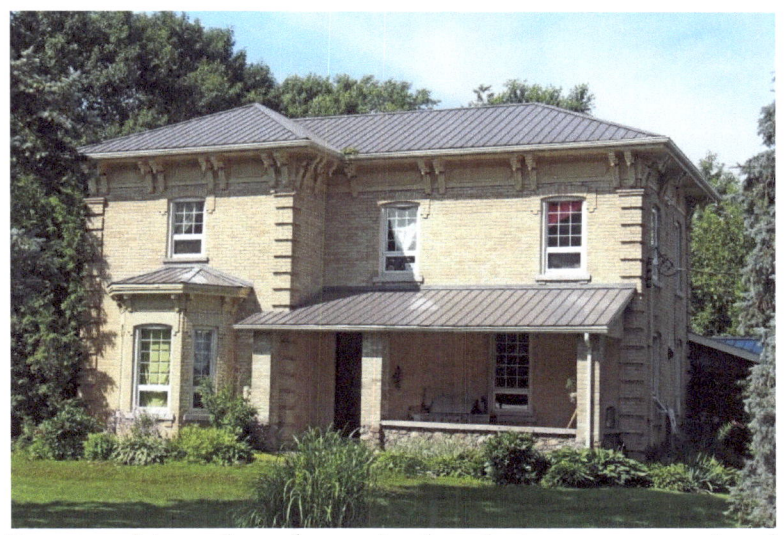

Italianate – hipped roof, cornice brackets, corner quoins, bay
window

Medina

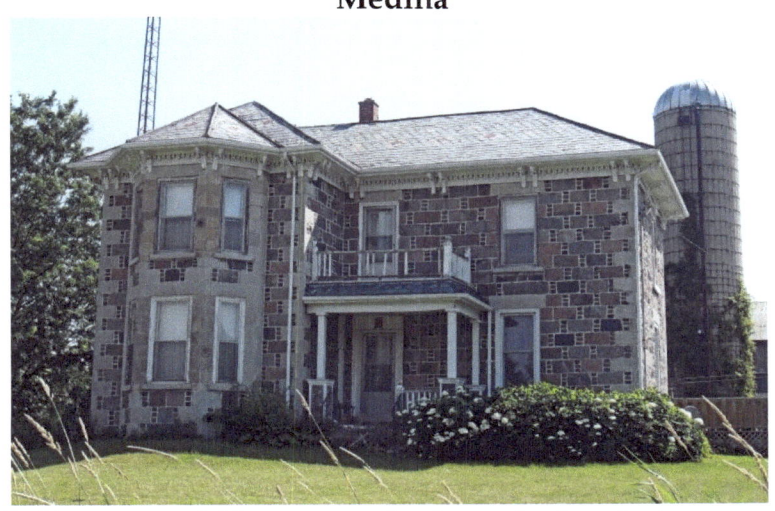

Italianate – cobblestone, paired cornice brackets, corner
quoins, two storey bay window

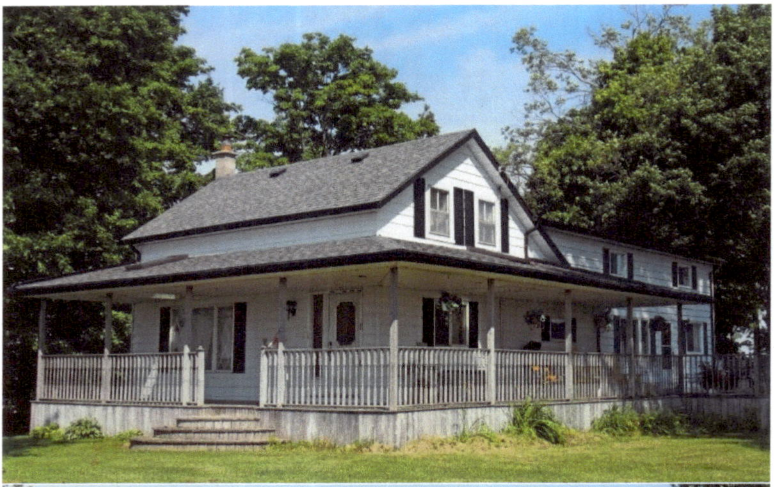

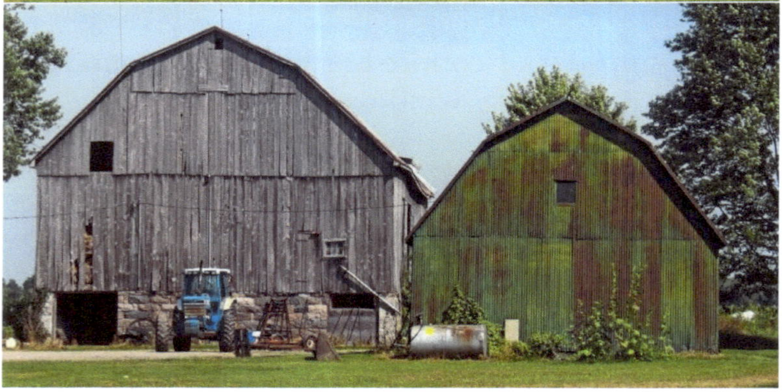

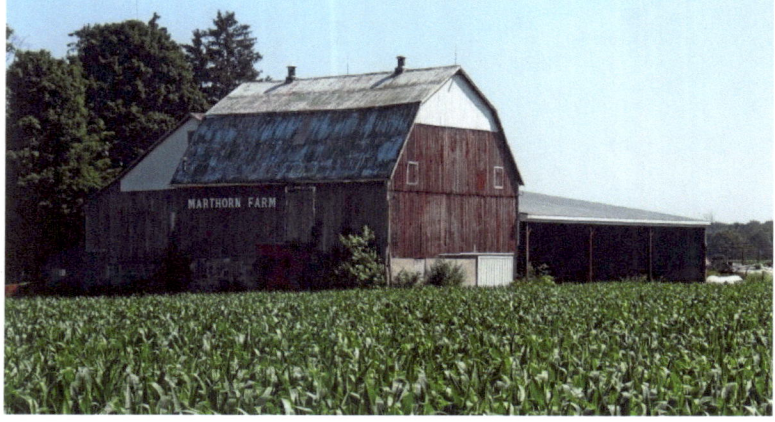

Gambrel roofs on barns

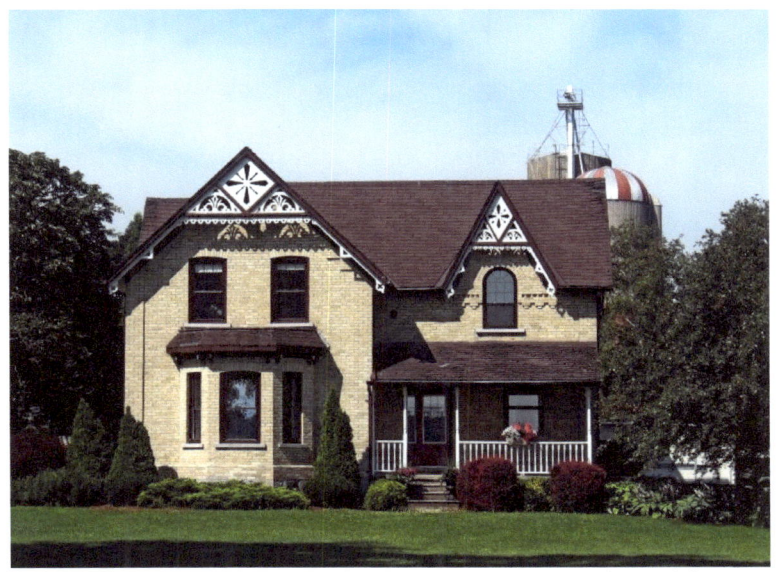

Gothic Revival - stenciling on the trim on the gables, bay window

Uniondale

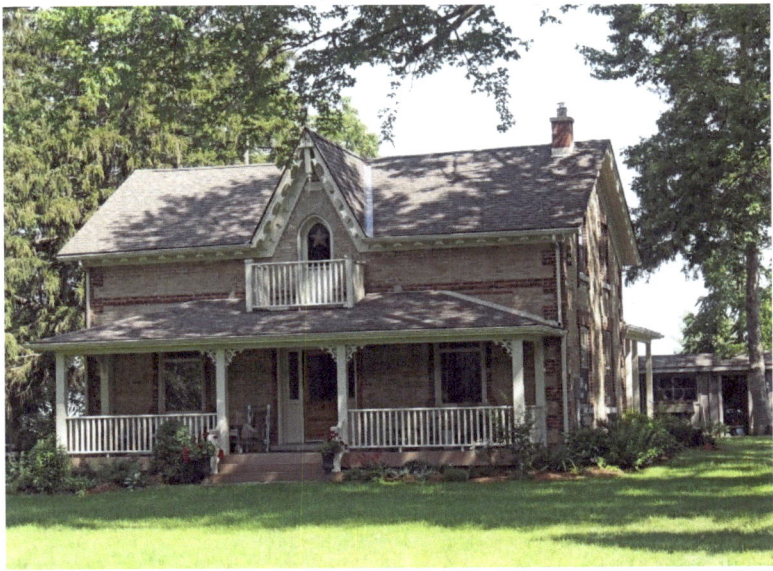

Gothic Revival, verge board trim and finial on gable, second floor balcony, dichromatic brickwork, corner quoins, bric-a-brac on porch

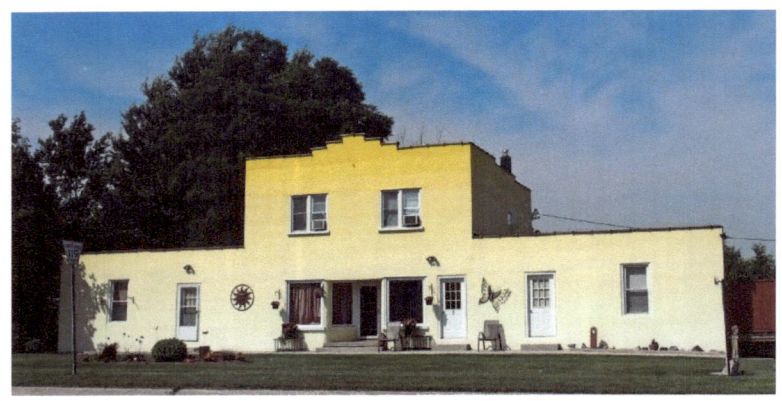

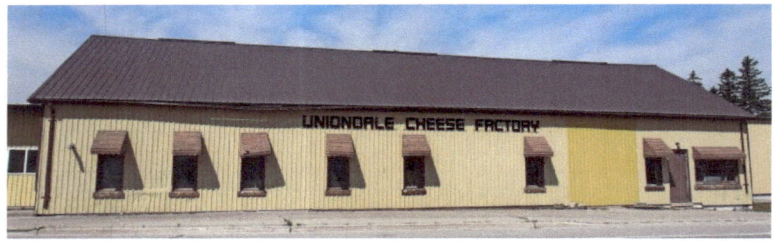

Uniondale Cheese Factory

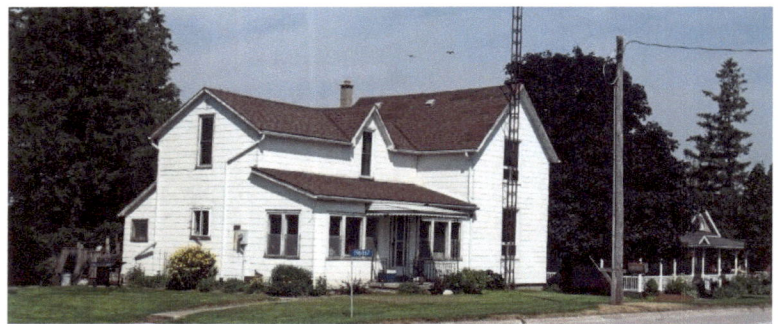

Gothic Revival

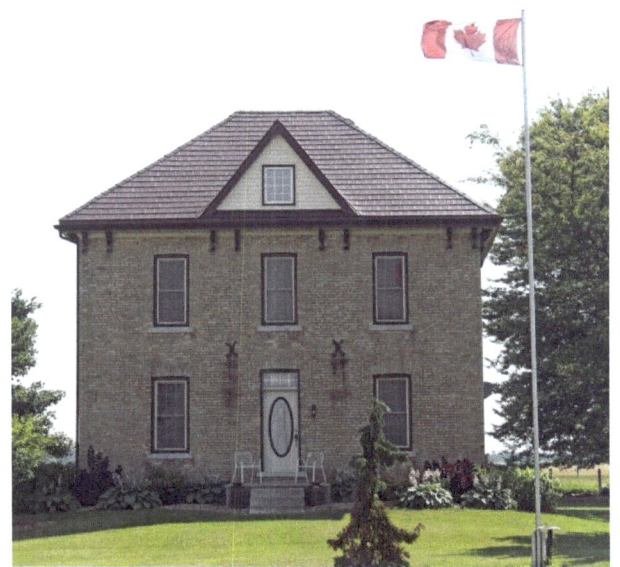

Italianate – hipped roof, paired cornice brackets

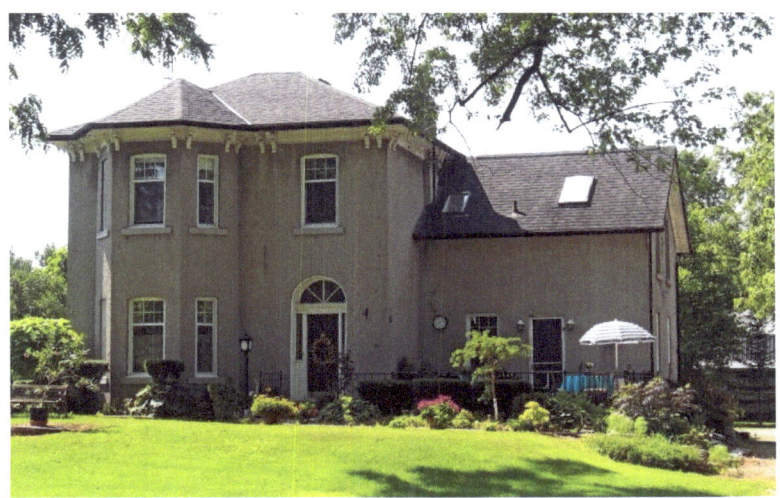

Italianate – hipped roof, paired cornice brackets, sidelights
and transom around main door, two-storey tower-like bay

Architectural Terms

Bay Window: A window that projects out from a wall, in a semicircular, rectangular, or polygonal design. Used frequently in Gothic and Victorian designs. Example: Kintore, Page 58	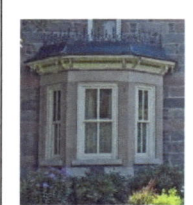
Brackets: a decorative or weight-bearing structural element which forms a right angle with one side against a wall and the other under a projecting surface such as an eave or roof. Example: 109 Dundas Street, Thamesford, Pg. 7	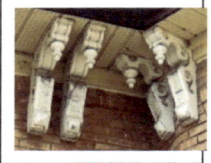
Buttress: a masonry structure built against or projecting from a wall which serves to support or reinforce the wall. In Canadian architecture, they are sometimes used for decoration. Example: 115 George Street, Page 31	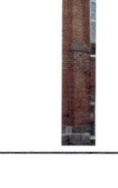
Cobblestone architecture: Refers to the use of cobblestones embedded in mortar as a method for erecting walls on houses and commercial buildings. Example: 115 George Street, Page 31	
Cornice: originally the wooden overhang of the roof. With the use of stone, brick, iron and steel, the cornice is any projecting shelf at the top of a ceiling or roof. They can be very decorative. Example: Kintore, Page 56	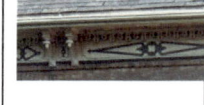
Dentil Moulding: an even series of rectangles used as ornamental decoration in cornices. Example: Kintore, Page 56	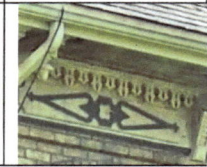

Dichromatic brickwork: the use of two colours of brick, tile or slate to decorate a façade. Example: Uniondale, Page 61	
Dormer: (French for "sleep") a gable end window that pierces through the plane of a sloping roof surface to create usable space in the top floor or attic of a building by adding headroom. Example: 134 Washington Street, Thamesford, Page 35	
Gable: the triangular portion of a wall between the edges of a sloping roof. Example: 174 Dundas Street, Thamesford, Page 11	
Gambrel Roof: a symmetrical two-sided roof with two slopes on each side; the upper slope is positioned at a shallow angle, while the lower slope is steep. It has vertical gable ends. Example: 155 Allen Street, Page 39	
Hipped Roof: a roof where all sides slope downwards to the walls with no gables. Example: Thamesford, Page 43	
Iron Cresting: A decorative ornament along the top of a roof. Iron cresting was popular in the Baroque era and also in Italianate, Victorian, Second Empire and Queen Anne styles of architecture. Example: Kintore, Page 58	

Keystones and Voussoirs: a voussoir is a wedge-shaped element used in building an arch. A keystone is the central stone that locks all the stones into position, allowing the arch to bear weight. A keystone is often enlarged and embellished. Example: George Street, Thamesford, Page 32	
Lancet Window: a tall, narrow window with a pointed arch at its top. Example: 115 George Street, Page 131	
Pediment: a triangular section above the horizontal structure (entablature), typically supported by columns. The inside of the triangle is called the tympanum. Example: 128 Delatre St. W., Thamesford, Pg. 24	
Quoin: masonry blocks at the corner of a wall, often a decorative feature, usually larger or of a different colour than the rest of the wall. Example: 205 Allen Street, Thamesford, Page 40	
Sidelight: a window, usually with a vertical emphasis, that flanks a door, and is often used to emphasize the importance of a primary entrance. **Transom Window:** the light above the doorway, also called a fanlight. Example: Uniondale, Page 63	
Verge board and Finial: also called bargeboards – hang from the projecting end of a roof and are often elaborately carved and ornamented. **Finial:** ornament added to the top of a gable, pinnacle, canopy or spire – a Gothic element. Example: Page 43	

Building Styles

Edwardian, 1900-1930 – This style bridges the ornate and elaborate styles of the Victorian era and the simplified styles of the 20th century. Balanced facades, simple roof lines, dormer windows, off-centre doorway, large front porches or verandahs with columns, Palladian window, pediment above the front steps, and smooth brick surfaces are its characteristics. Example: Washington Street, Page 33	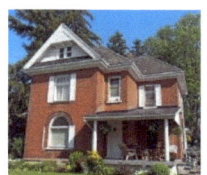
Gothic Revival, 1830-1890 – These decorative buildings have sharply-pitched gables with highly detailed verge boards, pointed-arch window openings, and dichromatic brickwork. It is a common style in Ontario. Example: 205 Allen Street, Thamesford, Pg. 40	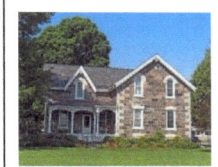
Italianate, 1850-1900 – was based on the architecture of the Tuscan country villas of Florentine elite. It is highly decorative coinciding with societies growing desire for ornaments. Some features are: wide, overhanging eaves; cupolas or belvederes; quoins, bay windows, frontispiece, columns or pilasters, double door with transom, cornice brackets (single or paired). Example: Kintore, Page 51	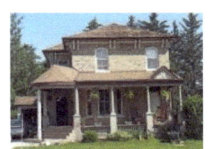

Tudor Revival – exposed timbers with stucco infill, multi-paned windows. Example: 127 Delatre Street West, Thamesford, Page 23	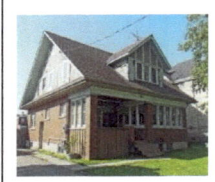
Vernacular/Traditional - 1638 - 1950 Influenced but not defined by a particular style, vernacular buildings are made from easily available materials and exhibit local design characteristics. Features include: rubble and stucco, fieldstone, hand-made brick or local stone construction; prominent window trim; gingerbread; quoins, end chimneys, large verandah, slightly irregular placement of window and door openings. Example: 200 Delatre Street West, Thamesford, Page 17	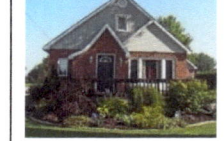

www.ingramcontent.com/pod-product-compliance
Lightning Source LLC
Chambersburg PA
CBHW040841180526
45159CB00001B/263